JES! Towards a Joint Effort Society

Frank van Empel
& Caro Sicking

JES! Towards a Joint Effort Society

First published as e-book, August 2013.
Publisher: Leanpub, Vancouver, Canada in cooperation with Studio nonfiXe, Vught, the Netherlands.
ISBN: 978.94.90665.104.

First printed edition, March 2014.
ISBN: 978.94.90665.111

Cover image: untitled, Joost Sicking, mixed media, 120x150cm, 1985, detail

nonfiXe
the power to differ

Table of Contents

Everywhere people ask: 'What can I actually do?' The answer is as simple as it is disconcerting: we can, each of us, work to put our inner house in order. The guidance we need for this work cannot be found in science or technology, the value of which utterly depends on the ends they serve; but it can still be found in the traditional wisdom of mankind.

E.F. Schumacher, Small is Beautiful, Economics as if People Mattered.

Preface

From Industrial to Spiritual Revolution

The belief that everyone, by virtue of her or his humanity, is entitled to certain unalienable freedoms is rooted in earlier tradition and documents of many cultures, but in the arenas of brute market forces human rights and needs have been completely misunderstood. They were formulated by higher Spirits. It took World War II as a beastly catalyst to propel human rights onto the global stage and into the global conscience. People like Robert Schuman – one of the founding fathers of the European Union – and Eleanor Roosevelt – co-initiator of the Universal Declaration of Human Rights – paved the way for the human rights movement. The moment of glory came in the sixties and seventies of the 20th century; hippies and other idealists claimed the power to change, former colonies liberated themselves from their Western rulers and the first steps towards a 'better' world were set in happy optimism. The backlash came almost immediately.

Ending the 1970's conservatism & competition in the political arena took over from idealism & cooperation. The dominant ideology of conservative politics and neo-liberal economics sang the same old song: enrich the rich, empower the empowered, after which the poor would rise from the Swamp of Poverty & Injustice in some miraculous manner. One of the tunes was called: supply side economics. Critics use the term 'trickle-down' economics. The main characteristics of supply side economics were large-scale tax cuts for individuals and corporations, deregulation of businesses and strong incentives for investment. This would lead to economic growth and an accumulation of wealth that would 'trickle down' the economy. Its proponents believed that making the rich richer eventually would help the poor because the benefits of an expanding economy would seep down to them. But, in fact, this last shackle of the chain got lost. And this is exactly what went wrong: Inequality grew like weed in the America's of Ronald Reagan.

Not only in the USA inequality grew during those years, all over the world disparities increased, despite humanitarian aid and development programs for the developing countries and for the poor and deprived. Especially on the African continent the population suffered and was unable to throw off the heritage of colonialism. Wars and famines raged, and still do, over the continent. Of the many theories and explanation on the causes, the socio-psychological analysis of John Kenneth Galbraith is much referred to. He published The Nature of Mass Poverty, at the eve of returning conservatism and neo-liberal economics, in 1979. Galbraith blamed e.g. accommodation for being one of the psychological forces of the poverty trap. The strategy to accommodate is a rational act, since improvement of the circumstances of life seems impossible to those who have suffered deprivation already for generations. No reasonable individual spills energy if there is no gain to expect from the effort. Accommodation can only be attacked by examples of successful escape. Migrants and revolutionaries are among the front soldiers that battle accommodation. They possess the will to succeed and show their peers that escape is possible, bringing energy and dynamics for change to the community.

Together all economic, political, ecological, socio-cultural and psychological developments have left 1,2 billion – and probably more – people in the world starving. They live on less than $1 a day. In Africa 46% of the population earns less than $1 a day.[1] It is one of the key problems and major societal threats of today.

JES! Towards a joint effort society is an attempt to contribute to the reduction of poverty and injustice. It advocates fundamental human freedoms and promotes to stimulate self-reliance. Professor of Philosophy (University of California) Paul Feyerabend provided the motto for this adventure: 'If we want to understand what is going on and if we want to change what displeases us then we have to know both the nature of the world and of human beings and we also have to know how they fit together'.[2]

So…
As opposed to the Historical Materialism of Karl Marx this book proposes Historical Spiritualism;
As opposed to Darwin's Evolution this book proposes Ecolution;

---

[1] 3.000.000.000 people have to live from $2 a day. World Bank, World Development Report, 2000-2001, 22
[2] Paul Feyerabend, The Tyranny of Science, Polity Press, 2011, p. 10

As opposed to a focus on Production & Consumption (Wants) this book stresses Needs & Opportunities;
As opposed to Galbraith's Affluent Society this book promotes a Joint Effort Society (JES) as part of a Spiritual & Moral Revolution. It is a natural follow up of Materialism, which dominated the last two hundred and fifty years.

Writing for a better world implies starting a dialogue with scholars who went there before, learn of their thoughts and meanings and make new combinations, and while doing so creating a fresh vision on what society needs today and tomorrow morning. While tomorrow afternoon, hopefully, somebody else will further the discussion. This person will reject parts of JES! and will embrace other pieces. She or he will create something new, again, and so on. This is the process of learning we call 'ecolution' and that has to go on and on to higher plateaus of awareness. This book is part of this neverending story.

Please join the dialogue: www.ecolutie.nl
Frank & Caro

Reader's guide

In the North life is focused on one purpose: bringing order in chaos. Still chaos is the rule, and so is disequilibrium. Order, linearity and balance are the exceptions. One strategy of politicians and policymakers is to break the rule and try to beat Nature. The other, more realistic, strategy is to get used to chaos and try to live with it. Chaos has a charming side to it. It leaves room for creation. Chaos is a system, like all others. It has structure. It is not pure anarchy. There are some ordering principles underneath all things. Things that present themselves as signs and clues to follow up on. One has to try and look at the *things behind the things*, the relations and at the patterns underneath.

A clarifying discovery was that of a rhizome. A rhizome is like a rootstock, a networked herb that grows underground with no other ordering principle than the search for fertile earth, water and sunlight. The rootstock is indestructible, unless the gardener uses chemicals or patiently, meticulously and continuously, keeps on weeding. Deleuze and Guattari wrote on the rhizome[3]: 'Let us summarize the principal characteristics of a rhizome: unlike trees or their roots, the rhizome connects any point to any other point, and its traits are not necessarily linked to traits of the same nature; it brings into play very different regimes of signs, and even nonsign states. The rhizome is reducible neither to the One nor the multiple.' 'It is composed not of units but of dimensions, or rather directions in motion. It has neither beginning nor end, but always a middle (milieu) from which it grows and which it overspills. It constitutes linear multiplicities with n dimensions having neither subject nor object, which can be laid out on a plane of consistency, and from which the One is always subtracted $(n - 1)$.'

JES! is a rhizome of words and concepts. There is no beginning, neither an end. You can plunge into it at every paragraph and find a dimension or a direction in motion. Always in motion, in development. All pages together form a network that may be hard to oversee or summarize, but that offers an intuitive vision for a

---

[3] Gilles Deleuze and Félix Guattari, a Thousand Plateaus, Capitalism and Schizophrenia, Continuum, 2008, p.23

direction society and individuals in that society can choose. Searching fertile grounds is done without a map, because as soon as the map is drawn the land has turned infertile or overcrowded. As soon as a society is described, developments have taken a different course and the society has changed. Only things that are dead and done can be rightfully described in a linear way, because the motion stopped, the 'thing' is finished, it has become something with a beginning and an end, history has entered. In that case the hindsight can do the trick, but for living organisms, under which we reckon all systems, just looking back is not sufficient for there is nothing linear between the past, the present and the future.

The rhizome needs to be approached from the middle, which can be at any place of the network. To find it we need to develop at least an understanding of how it works. Understanding goes beyond knowledge or information, although these are required. Understanding needs context too as well as experience. All these elements come together in intuition, which enables a person to dance with systems. Dancing is the only effective way to interfere, as Donella Meadows stated.[4]

A person can start to understand her or his surroundings and circumstances once knowledge and information are embedded in a context. A context that changes with time and place. It needs to be researched carefully before applying ecolution.

The theory of ecolution introduces a method and toolbox for change. Please keep in mind that this is a process, an ongoing development. The toolbox is just as dynamic as reality is. It contains concepts, which are plans for action that are variable and multiple. Each person, community or organization can think of their own. Seven criteria to select concepts support the choice for constructive plans.

The match of context and concept offers content, it stirs the mind to change and gives meaning to the plan. The idea becomes reality and evolves, new ideas sprout, unknown territory will be discovered. Every time this occurs, society develops towards a higher ecological, economic, societal and psychological level in the direction of a joint effort society.

---

[4] Donella Meadows, Thinking in Systems, Earthscan, 2009

Featuring JES!

We will focus on change and finding solutions for unsustainable developments. Some new terms are introduced in order to be able to start with a fresh vocabulary.

This conceptual framework originates from Only Winners[5] and was developed to research and successfully implement regional sustainable development. JES! applies it on global scale in order to find a different societal and political engagement model that can be of help to change-agents, organizations, communities and societies. As you will find out in the following chapters the proposed model is multi-leveled, designed for both individual and collective change. All starts with awareness and a vision of the direction in which a person and / or a community want to move. Checks and balances to make sure that this direction is a path towards human wellbeing with respect for nature, can be found e.g. in the paragraph 'Selecting concepts'.

The conceptual framework introduces the prima *donna's* of the theory as if they were actors in a play. They should be perceived as evolving characters that cannot be pinned down to a single definition. Words and concepts change from time to time, grow entropy, get lost and are found again, just like people. Several descriptions are compressed into a few razor blade definitions by means of a first introduction. These focus on human beings, which does not mean that animals, plants, dead materials, nature, earth, art, science and philosophy are not important. The World is also thèir stage, and each plays its', her or his role, and adds value to the whole.

The rhizome that is metaphorical to the structure of JES!, as explained in the reader's guide, offers the opportunity to hand out a sneak preview of the main definitions here and now.

JES = Joint Effort Society = a new political engagement model and free association of individuals. All contribute, cooperate and co-create according to their ability and out of free will and all reap the

---

[5] Allemaal Winnen, regionale duurzame ontwikkeling (Ecolutie), Bakker & Van Empel, Erasmus University Rotterdam, Studio nonfiXe, April 2012

fruits. A joint effort society has a healthy relationship with nature, understands the interconnectedness and reciprocity of systems and aims at the wellbeing of all people, here and now, there and later.

Ecolution = the dynamics of societal, cultural, economic, ecological and psychological powers towards a joint effort society.

Ecolution means developing, transcending and exploring:
A natural development towards a system that is in balance - economic, ecological, psychological and social;
A continuous transition towards a higher level of economic, ecological, psychological and societal development;
An expedition into the future, in search of behaviour, technology / institutionalization and governance that ensure a livable planet & lead to higher levels of awareness, which help individuals and groups of people to rise to their higher potentialities.

The Matrix = a dynamic toolbox and evaluation method that stimulates people to move systematically in the direction of higher levels of awareness and wellbeing.

Deconstruction = disordering the status quo

Concept = a design for action

Context

Introduction

The following paragraphs sketch a historical context to discuss how the global community arrived at the situation of today. Why did we install the economic system the way we did? Are there other possibilities and what do we need, to re-install systems that help us to construct a society in which we want to live, i.e. communities that join efforts to live in peace and concordance with nature and individual wellbeing?

There are opportunities and destructive systems can be reinstalled (Some avant-garde groups and individuals have already turned to different organizing principles). In the following paragraphs neo-classical economic axioms are discussed and replaced with a different set of assumptions.

The main required change is that of replacing competition (fed and sustained by neo-classical economics) with cooperation.

The Run-up

'Zwei Seelen wohnen, ach! in meiner Brust,' the famous German writer and poet Johann Wolfgang von Goethe's tragic hero Faust exclaimed. Faust is symbolic for the primal problem of human existence: being torn between two opposing, seemingly incompatible Worlds. Von Goethe's contemporary, Adam Smith - the Godfather of all economists – struggled with a similar dichotomy in his two masterpieces. Seventeen years before The Wealth of Nations (TWN) Smith as a professor of Moral Philosophy at the University of Glasgow wrote The Theory of Moral Sentiments (TMS). The original work arose from Smith's lectures to students. If The Wealth of Nations is the Yang of modern economics, The Theory of Moral Sentiments can be called the Yin. Both works must be taken together and considered as one. Quote from TMS: 'How selfish whatsoever man may be supposed, there are evidently some principles in his nature, which interest him in the fortune of others and render their happiness necessary to him, though he derives nothing from it except the pleasure of seeing it. Of this kind is pity or compassion, the emotion we feel for the misery of others, when we either see it, or are made to conceive it in a very lively manner. That we often derive sorrow from the sorrow of others, is a matter of fact too obvious to require any instances to prove it...'

In The Theory of Moral Sentiments Smith investigated the empathic part of human nature. In The Wealth of Nations he researched man's selfish side. TWN probably is among the most misquoted of economic theories. Most economic works confine to reciting the sentence on the butchers', brewers' & bakers' self- interest. Smith was much more concerned on the effects of selfishness and greed in a free market than most neoliberal economists want us to believe. Adam Smith: 'When a man of fortune spends his revenu chiefly in hospitality, he shares the greater part of it with his friends and companions; but when he employs it in purchasing such durable commodoties, he often spends the whole upon his own person, and gives nothing to anybody without an equivalent. The latter species of expense, therefore, especially when directed to frivolous objects, the little ornaments of dress and furniture, jewels, trinkets, gewgaws, frequently indicates, not only a trifling, but a base and selfish disposition. All that I mean is, that the one sort of expense, as it always occasions some accumulation of valuable commodities, as it is more favourable to private frugality, and, consequently, to the increase of public capital, and as it maintains productive, rather than unproductive hands, conduces more than the other to the growth of public opulence.'[6]

Despite the paragraphs similar to the above he wrote in TWN, talking about 'prodigals and projectors' while referring to excessive searchers for profits, Smith is considered the Nestor of the neoclassical movement that is dominant in contemporary economy. The other side that promotes a socio-economical approach and some of whom hold a different view on the legacy of Adam Smith, represents famous names as well, such as: Michal Kalecki, John Maynard Keynes, Amartya Sen, Joseph Schumpeter, John Kenneth Galbraith, E.F. Schumacher, Manfred Max-Neef and P.R. Dubashi. Their thinking is part of the economic foundations under the joint effort society.

The latter movement's vision is much more on track when we look for what the world needs. It is of great importance to get a grip on environmental and social issues and to come up with sound solutions for global problems. 'A whole new environmental economics needs to be developed going far beyond the narrow vision of mainstream micro-economics in order to come to grips with the issues relating to

---

[6] Adam Smith, the Wealth of Nations, Penguin books, 1976, p.449

"sustainable development",' Prof. P.R. Dubhashi from GOA University, India, wrote.[7] His fellow countryman, Nobel prizewinner, Amartya Sen, described the selfish calculating neo-classical economists as 'rational fools'.

The 'narrow vision' of mainstream micro-economics has to do with its unsound assumptions, its preoccupation with the short run rather than the long run, with much more static state than dynamic changes, with money and wealth, rather than meaningfulness and wellbeing. Dubhashi: 'The preoccupation with theoretical and mathematical equations rather than the problems of the day has reduced Economics to "esoteric[8] irrelevance".'

Dubashi attacked the axioms[9] of neo-classical (micro) economics[10], which has been dominant in designing economic, financial, political, institutional, governmental and personal strategies for the future, for more than three decades.

The concept of 'homo-economicus', the individual economic agent whether consumer or producer - making choices or taking decisions, is a faulty one. An individual does not exist in isolation. He or she is a member of a family and society and his or her choices and decisions are influenced by interpersonal relationships and community values. The economic activity is embedded in a web of social institutions.[11]

The assumption that an individual makes 'rational' choices and takes 'rational decisions' is not valid. The behaviour of the individual is influenced by many factors including moral and ethical considerations and is not purely 'hedonist' in character. 'Impulse buying', spontaneous consumption decisions, adventure and desire for the unknown are not always 'rational'. But they do characterize

---

[7] P.R. Dubashi, Critique of Neo-classical Economics, Mainstream, Vol. XLVI, No. 19. Prof. Dubashi is former Vice-Chancelor, GoA University and erstwhile Secretary, Government of India.

[8] Esoteric means: likely to be understood or enjoyed by only a few people with a special knowledge or interest (OALD)

[9] An axiom is a rule or principle that most people, including the mainstream of economists, believe to be true. (OALD)

[10] 'Neoclassical' is a term that's used for several kinds of economic approaches focusing on the determination of prices in markets. Prices are the result of a confrontation of supply and demand in a certain market.

[11] Prof. Dr. P.R. Dubhashi, Critique of Neo-classical Economics, Mainstream Weekly, Vol. XLVI, No 19, p. 8, 2008

individual decisions.

The assumptions relating to a perfectly competitive market are inconsistent with the conditions in the real world. One of the assumptions is that there are innumerable buyers and sellers none of whom, individually or as a group, is able to influence the market. In the actual world however, there are conditions of monopoly, oligopoly and imperfect competition based on differentiated products. As J. K. Galbraith pointed out, today's corporations are so powerful that with the aid of advertisements and money power they are able to reverse the proposition that supply is according to demand. Corporations manipulate demand to be in accordance with supply. Already in 1776 Adam Smith was aware of the shortcomings of the markets. 'In reality,' he wrote in his Inquiry, 'high profits tend much more to raise the price of work than high wages.' (...) 'Our merchants and master-manufacturers complain much of the bad effects of high wages in raising the price, and thereby lessening the sale of their goods both at home and abroad. They say nothing concerning the bad effects of high profits. They are silent with regard to the pernicious effects of their own gains. They complain only of those of other people.'[12]
The assumption of 'perfect knowledge' is not valid either. Consumers are often ill informed about the products and services they buy, not in the least due to the misinformation marketeers spread using their billion dollars advertisement budgets.

We have to take the critiques on the axioms of neo-classical economics seriously, since the systems we installed are running rampant and many a system is rooted in the neo-classical thinking model. For instance the primacy of the economy over ecology, society and individual freedoms are results of this choice. However, today the limits are clearly being set by ecology and society. Resource depletion and extreme poverty are threatening the world order. Authorities lose command over the masses.

A rather young science, social psychology, seems to agree with the criticasters of neoclassical economics on important points and offers solutions or parts of solutions.

---

[12] Adam Smith, The Wealth of Nations, Pelican Classics, p.200-201

A cooperative versus a competitive process

Professor in social psychology Morton Deutsch was born in 1920 as the youngest of four boys in a Jewish American family. The young Morton was continuously trying to keep up with, or rather, get ahead of, his older brothers. He grew to be a competitive teenager that enrolled City College of New York at the age of fifteen, two and half years younger then the other students. At that time he started to notice how good it felt when he won, while others – the losers – felt bad, or ashamed. On the other hand, he himself too felt stupid and unworthy when he lost some competition. This is how his fascination for the dichotomy competition-cooperation started.

And gasoline fed the fire. The times were frantic and often destructive: economic crises, rising unemployment rates, brutal civil wars like the one in Spain against dictator Franco and, growing racism, Nazism and anti-Semitism. Then competition showed its' ugliest face and turned into a worldwide deadly conflict.

After the War had broken out, Morton Deutsch enlisted as combat pilot. 'I flew in thirty bombing missions against the Germans. During combat I saw many of our planes as well as German planes shot down, and I also saw the massive damage inflicted by our bombs and those of the Royal Air Force on occupied Europe and Germany. Moreover, being stationed in England, I saw the great destruction wreaked by the German air raids and felt the common apprehensions while sitting in air-raid shelters during German bombings. Although I had no doubt of the justness of the war against the Nazis, I was appalled by its destructiveness.'

Morton Deutsch spent most of his working years on trying 'to understand the fundamental features of cooperative and competitive relations and the consequences of these different types of interdependencies in a way that would be generally applicable to the relations among individuals, groups, or nations'. He found out that when dealing with a problem a cooperative process appeared to be more productive than a competitive process.

Deutsch came up with the crude law of social relations. This law explains 'that the characteristic processes and effects elicited by a given type of social relationship (cooperative or competitive) also tend to elicit that type of social relationship'. Deutsch: 'Thus cooperation induces and is induced by a perceived similarity in beliefs and attitudes, a readiness to be helpful, openness in communication, trusting and friendly attitudes, sensitivity to common interests and de-emphasis of opposed interests, an orientation toward enhancing mutual power rather than power differences, and so on. Similarly, competition induces and is induced by the use of tactics of coercion, threat, or deception; attempts to enhance the power differences between oneself and the other; poor communication; minimization of the awareness of similarities in values and increased sensitivity to opposed interests; suspicion and hostile attitudes: the importance, rigidity, and size of the issues in conflict, and so on.'[13]

In other words, when parties invest in trust, communication, getting to know each other and each other's motives, the competitive attitude may change into a cooperative one. And, a cooperative attitude leads to a more productive solution of the problem.[14]

The assumptions of the theory of ecolution

The shortcomings of neoclassical economic approaches that were elaborated in the Run-up combined with the insights of Social Psychology lead to the assumptions on which the theory of ecolution is based. There are five of them:

1. The Economy is embedded in the Ecology;
2. People have rational as well as irrational preferences;
3. Individuals and firms are not one-dimensionally focused on profit, but definitely want to add value to environmental, spatial and social development. They share their ups and downs with the local community and with society at large;
4. People act in line with the multitude on the base of limited information;
5. Individual people and firms work together out of self-interest. *What's in it for me?* is a reasonable question. After all mostly 'working together' gives a bigger plus than rivalry, opposing and

---

[13] Morton Deutsch, A personal Perspective on Social Psychology, 1999
[14] Methods such as the Method Holistic Participation and the Mutual Gains Approach build towards such cooperative attitude between involved, as can be read further on in this book.

competition. If not, there still may be enough gains in it for everyone.

The Force of the matrix[15]

All the world's a stage,
And all the men and women merely players: They have their exits and their
entrances; And one man in his time plays many parts,
William Shakespeare

The five assumptions on which the theory of ecolution is based call for a different household management than the type neo-liberal economists have been promoting. Economy is put back to the place where it belongs: embedded in and supportive of social, ecological and psychological needs. Ecolution as described in the chapter Featuring JES! is a three-layered concept: a natural development, a continuous transition and an expedition into the future. All three layers are dynamic and fit for change. The concept aims at developing towards a higher ecological, socio-cultural, economic and psychological level. The question is how to bring this about? The truthful cliché is that change is perpetual. Although a rather quick reversal needs to be brought about by force or, by a main concept in the conceptual framework of JES! called deconstruction. Deconstruction leads to chaos, the system that leaves room for creation.

It is wise to encourage deconstruction and its' agents, the dissidents, for every system develops slack, which is the presentiment of going destructive. Diversity, dissent and variety keep a system healthy, although its' natural tendency is to smoothen differences and smother critics.
To find the course a society, group, organization, a person (or even the whole world) set out to, and to explore which course is desired a matrix is developed.

This matrix is the compass and evaluating tool of the theory of ecolution. The figure visualizes the dynamics of developments. The

---

[15] This chapter is inspired among others by works of Gregory Bateson, E.F. Schumacher, Gilles Deleuze and Félix Guattari, as well as on the thesis Allemaal Winnen, Bakker & Van Empel, Rotterdam, 2012

dynamic character is emphasized by the timeline on the horizontal axis that shows the stage a development is in: destruction phase, deconstruction phase and construction phase. This matrix is first introduced in the next paragraph together with a symbol for ecolution that expresses dynamics and can be found in the deconstruction phase. It will be further elaborated on in the coming paragraphs and the next chapter The Theory of Ecolution.

Change is the essence of life. Most changes just happen, apparently without human interference. Some changes can be manipulated. Some need force, like the birth of a child. What counts is the change itself. Change stimulates resilience, flexibility and sensitivity to change. Those are lessons from biology and psychology that can be adopted by social science and economy.

Ecolution[16] is a catalyst for change. It is about the creative destruction of attitudes, technologies, institutions, decisionmaking, procedures, protocols and forces of habit that are taken for granted and have become a burden instead of a blessing for the individual, as well as for the communities he or she is part of. Ecolution paves the way for something completely different, something better then before. Ecolution is a conscious, though not always directed, action for improvement. It happens during, or causes, times of chaos, turmoil and disorder that we call the deconstruction phase. Before that, there was either destruction or construction. The natural course of systems, networks and rhizomes consists of growth and entropy. Sometimes the destruction stops and becomes construction without interference. Such self-organizational pattern is better off without meddling. At other moments countervailing powers are needed to turn the tide. Then ecolution has to be stimulated.

Ecolution is visualized by a dynamic symbol:

---

[16] The theory of ecolution and subsequent the conceptual framework, toolbox and matrix originate from *Allemaal Winnen*, Bakker & Van Empel, Erasmus University, Rotterdam, April 2012.

Exploration and experimentation lead to the lever points of a system and how to perform ecolution. And if it is a success, share it, so others in likewise situations can apply it too.

In order to find in which direction a person, system or society is developing, we look for patterns[17] that we try to catch in words. People, systems and organizations are moving from one phase or state to another. When we perform ecolution we search for concepts to describe what is going on and to point out where we want to go from here.

A concept is an idea or principle that is connected with something abstract. It is also a design for concrete action. Concepts are the building blocks of theory intended to explain why something happens or exists, as a run-up to practice, or they are intended to inspire.

The concept can be: biomimicry The concept can be: no waste
The concept can be: cooperation
The concept can be: justice, or mercy, or both - freedom, or order, or both.

Ideas, concepts and theories that may be useful to turn a destructive movement into construction, or to prevent constructive developments turning into bad ones, are classified in a matrix.
The horizontal axis (X) describes time and stage of the development. On the vertical axis (Y) three solutionfinding clusters can be found:

1. Behaviour;
2. Technology and Institutionalization;
3. Decisionmaking.

We can design action in all three solutionfinding clusters by filling the matrix with concepts: How to change destruction into construction? How to prevent constructive developments from growing destructive? Which concept(s) will be chosen, depends on the context.

---

[17] Douglas Flemons, PhD., May the Pattern be With You, Cybernetics and Human Knowing, Vo. 12, nos.1-2,--.91-101

	Destruction phase	Deconstruction phase	Construction phase
Behaviour		◎	
Technology/Institutionalization		◎	
Decisionmaking		◎	

When we observe eco-systems, social and economic systems, we have to conclude that these all are in the phase of destruction. Human behaviour, the mainstream technologies, the way we designed procedures and protocols as well as how decisions are made (or avoided) all three clusters can be found in the destruction phase of development. Climate change, air and water pollution, dependency on fossil fuels, mass-poverty, violence, dictatorial regimes, slavery, lack of freedom in general, etc, prove the inability of the human race to behave, invent and decide for a cleaner, healthier and better world. These are the forces that hamper progress.

Politicians, business leaders, trade unions, representatives of all kinds of institutions, scientists, all those we look up to for solutions, are doomed to fail, because systems, networks and societies have grown too big and too complex to steer top down. That is why we - in the slipstream of the economists, E.F. Schumacher and Manfred Max-Neef - opt for 'economics as if people mattered'[18] and 'human scale development'[19]. Such alternative development theories aim at generating capacity for more self-reliance.

Human scale development assumes an economic system that brings consumption closer to local production. Agriculture and small-scale production facilities around town and craftsmanship, service providers and city-farmers in the city make it unnecessary to transport goods thousands of kilometres.

Human-scale development also presumes direct and participatory democracy, instead of the current representative democracy, that does

[18] E.F. Schumacher, Small is Beautiful, Economics as if People Mattered
[19] Manfred Max-Neef, Human Scale Development, The Apex Press,1991

not satisfy the needs of most people. The new role for politics and government is: to encourage creative solutions to grow from the bottom up.

Conceptualize

In order to set for a direction two opposites are placed in the matrix. The dichotomy makes it conceivable for the human mind to find an answer. An example is the dichotomy that fascinated Morton Deutsch:

Competition →  → Cooperation

How do we get from competition to cooperation? Which concepts can be of help? It is important to use the genius of the group involved to find solutions. A group of people usually knows more than just one individual. John Kolstoe called this creative genius. 'Creative genius includes the ability to see things from different viewpoints; to use the old in new ways; to connect familiar but unrelated things; to combine information from the recesses of the mind with the perceptions of the physical senses; to go beyond the shackles of traditional thinking.'[20] Therefore consultation is one of the concepts to explore and experiment with.

Here the concept ecolution shall be discussed. Then the expedition moves on to the context and several old and new concepts that need to be addressed. Together context and concept create meaning (content) as the architectural approach of Bernard Tschumi showed.[21] Tschumi inspired to look at reality in terms of context, concept and content. 'As a starting point,' he wrote, 'it is useful to look at three basic ways in which concept and context may relate:

1. Indifference, whereby the idea and its siting are superbly ignorant of one another - a kind of accidental collage in which both coexist but do not interact. Poetic juxtapositions or irresponsible impositions may result;

---

[20] John Kolstoe, Developing Genius, Georg Ronald Publisher Ltd, 1995, p. 13.
[21] Bernard Tschumi, Event Cities 3, Concept vs. Context, MIT Press, Cambridge, 2004.

2. Reciprocity, whereby the architectural concept and its context interact closely with one another, in a complimentary way, so that they seem to merge seamlessly into a single continuous entity;
3. Conflict, whereby the architectural concept is strategically made to clash with its context, in a battle of opposites in which both protagonists may need to negotiate their own survival.

'These three strategies – indifference, reciprocity, and conflict - are all valid architectural approaches. Selecting the appropriate strategy for a given project is part of the concept.' The strategies Tschumi discussed can be defined as planned relationships. The relationship between the context and the concept then determines the meaning (content).

This meaning can be a context in itself as well and become connected to a concept again and give birth to a new meaning. This way the amount of relationships and changing roles accumulate, making things (and systems) complex.
In other words, it is all about relationships and connections between systems (people are considered systems as well), inside systems and among them. These relationships (contexts and concepts) that give (content) meaning to something - to a word, an idea, an object, a place – define the world in which we live. The complexity is so dynamic that no linear or static model can capture it. Still we, men and women, like to intervene when we observe something going wrong. We can use our intuition and we can try to develop dynamic models to enhance our understanding and awareness.

At the finish, the best and worst practices are shared and the context is wrapped around the Joint Effort Society to give it meaning. The exercise helps to understand the world and to choose actions for change.

Why ecolution?
Ecolution can be defined as a development, transcendence and/or as an expedition to the future within and among interconnected ecological, economic, socio-cultural and psychological fields. The attractiveness as well as the complexity of ecolution is that it is dynamic (nonfixe). The discourse on development needs a fresh approach. The new concept is meant to inspire and replace worn- out

paradigms and concepts such as sustainability. Ecolution is wider because it incorporates the present, a development as well as the future. Whereas sustainability is a contradictio in terminis. It is a word that carries opposite meanings – for all living organisms and systems suffer from entropy (everything falls apart) and the materials that come close to being sustainable, such as plastics, are part of the problem the adepts of sustainability want to solve.

Ecolution is not confined within a strict frame or definition on purpose and is based upon the following key concepts or elements:

• The three capitals - economy, ecology and society - are equivalent;
• Every society, community, organization, group or individual can apply ecolution;
• Change is perpetual, always and everywhere;
• The goal is continuous progress towards another (higher) level of development.

Ecolution is part of a conceptual framework within which people work together and strive to higher levels of awareness, beyond their basic instincts like fear, anger, jealousy, greed and aggression. As a human being we can be consciously aware of our emotions and choose not to identify with them. 'The road to brain wellness begins with awareness. It also ends in awareness, and awareness allows every step along the way. In the brain, energy flows where awareness goes.'[22]

Thinking of concepts to take off to the construction phase is stretching the mind for possibilities and opening up to positive developments. It is a practice in awareness. According to Chopra and Tanzi 'the brain is multidimensional, in order to allow any experience to occur'. The human brain is incredibly resilient. It gives people the capability, in their thoughts, feelings and actions, 'to develop in any direction they choose'. In other words: everything is possible.

The Super Brain can override even the most instinctive fears: fears of failure, humiliation, rejection, old age, sickness and death. We humans suffer in our inner world and so, we may decide to stop worrying and

[22] Deepak Chopra & Rudolph E. Tanzi, Super Brain, Rider, 2012, p. 38

stress higher states of awareness, like understanding, wisdom, compassion, participation, love and empathy. For example: Justice is a denial of mercy, and mercy is a denial of justice. Only a higher force can reconcile these opposites: wisdom. The problem cannot be solved, but wisdom can transcend it, as Schumacher taught. 'Societies,' he wrote, 'need stability ánd change, tradition ánd innovation, public interest ánd private interest, planning ánd laissez-faire, order and freedom, growth and decay. Everywhere society's health depends on the simultaneous pursuit of mutually opposed activities or aims. The adoption of a final solution means a kind of death sentence for man's humanity and spells either cruelty or dissolution, generally both.

'Divergent problems offend the logical mind, which wishes to remove tension by coming down on one side or the other, but they provoke, stimulate, and sharpen the higher human faculties, without which man is nothing but a clever animal.'[23]

A polycentric world

The human race cannot be covered by one blanket. There is no solution that fits all. The diverse women and men that populate the world each live their own reality built up by beliefs, experiences, misfortunes and luck, by education, health, their environment and activities in daily life.

Individuals communicate through facebook or twitter, and / or gather physical to build up a 'multitude of resistance'. The multitude attracts and binds people. In the complexity of modern times people act on rational as well as irrational bases in line with the multitude. Call it intuition, herd behaviour or guts. People cannot oversee the whole, maybe they cannot reach fellow Musketeers, but they feel their energy or just know what to do, like birds of passage flying in formation.

The context within which all choices of individuals as well as organizations have to be made, can be understood and changed through concepts that replace old paradigms for new ones to give meaning (content).
Gilles Deleuze and Félix Guattari provided quite an accurate

---

[23] E.F. Schumacher, A guide for the Perplexed, Harper Perennial, 1977, p.127/128

description of the current context that can be applied on the global level. They spoke of rhizomes, underground and wild growing networks of creeping stems that pop up from the earth at convenient places for the plant to grow. These rootstocks are the metaphor for bottom-up developments that cannot be erased.[24]

The power of one

Rhizomes symbolize what the former president of the Czech Republic Václav Havel called 'the power of the powerless.'[25]

A recent example of the power of the powerless is shown in the Arab Countries in December 2010. A young Tunisian that kept his family alive by selling fruits and vegetables on the street set himself on fire. The story that spread was that he did so out of protest to oppression and abuse by local authorities. This story was fast and widely distributed by social media such as facebook and twitter. The information helped to catalyze and empowered people to openly protest in Tunisia and more broadly within other countries in the Arab world against their ruling classes. The Arab people joined each other and massively demanded freedom, dignity, jobs and equality for the first time in history.

Two years later, in 2012, a fourteen minute movie trailer of bad artistic quality set the Muslim community aflame again. Worldwide. The film, released on Youtube, defamed the Prophet Mohammed[26]. The exploration of freedom of expression in relation to religion got a sour setback. It cost the lives of people who had nothing to do with it. This event showed how fast images and ideas can be spread, how fragile we as a global community are and how one networked individual or organization can have an impact, for the better, and for the worse.

Looking for patterns

Our contemporary confusing context of interconnected social, ecological and economic systems in which countries, regions and individuals are embedded, needs concepts and models to make it

---

[24] Deleuze & Guattari, A Thousand Plateaux, The Continuum Publishing Company, Edition 2004, p. 23.

[25] Steve Crawshaw & John Jackson, Small Acts of Resistance, Sterling Publishing Co., 2010, p. ix.

[26] Innocence of Muslims by Sam Bacile, a pseudonym.

possible to develop from dictatorships to free societies, from industrial structures towards post-industrial, ecological production and organization structures, as Rüdiger Lutz c.s. claimed in Innovations-Ökologie.[27] New broadly supported paradigms are needed to enable mankind to redesign systems and structures that support truly sustainable - people, planet & profit - development. For example, reframing the paradigm 'Growth is good' can lead to the perspective 'Voluntary Simplicity'.

Continuous framing and reframing helps people to recognize the non-linear character of developments, thoughts and events.[28] In order to change old paradigms for new ones on large scale, a philosophic framework, a grand and inspiring story is required. A story that sets appealing goals for individuals and organizations. A recommendation made in the thesis Only Winners: 'Here may very well lay a new task for regional governments that are close enough to know the local community and its' key players and are able to connect people on mutual goals'.[29]

Thinking different

The planet when left to its' own devices is a sustainable system. Society is a system, so is the economy and the power balance between nations. All relationships are systems, like a woman's mind or a man's body. Religions are systems, just as this text is. Google is a system, and facebook as well. Systems define our world. These sisters of Hydra are not easily defeated, even if we wish to do so. Their many-headedness leads to benefits or destruction, depending on which head you look at. Systems, as institutions, tend to develop slack at some point, when the reason for existence is long forgotten and the system or institution becomes an organism solely struggling for its own existence, applying rules for the rules, not for the people, using protocols and procedures that obstruct rather than create possibilities and opportunities.

---

[27] Rüdiger Lutz, Fritjof Capra, Ernest Callenbach & Sandra Marburg, Innovations-Ökologie, page 11
[28] Rein and Schön, Reframing policy discourse eds., F. Fisher and J. Forrester, London UCL Press, 1993, p.146
[29] Only Winners, Allemaal Winnen, Martin Bakker & Frank van Empel, Erasmus University, April 2012. The basics of the ecolution theory, toolbox and conceptual framework originate from Only Winners.

Travelling with the Hydra means following ones intuition. System thinkers like Donella Meadows and MIT's Jay Forrester admitted that intuition plays an important role in coming to grips with systems. Meadows wrote: 'We have built up intuitively, without analysis, often without words, a practical understanding of how these systems work, and how to work with them.'[30]

Forrester and Meadows showed that it is possible to change the structure of systems by using so called 'leverage points' - places in the system where a small change can lead to a large shift in behaviour. In order to find these points people have to be wise. They have to use their brains as well as their intuition. Forrester warned that although people deeply involved in a system often know intuitively where to find leverage points, more often than not they push the change in the wrong direction.

So Forrester relied not only on his gut feeling but used a computer to make some calculations. In 1971 that was very innovative, most computers were huge, slow and dumb. Nevertheless Forrester made a computer model and came out with a clear leverage point: growth.[31] 'Growth has costs as well as benefits, and we typically don't count the costs,' explained Meadows, who worked with Forrester on the growth-project in the early seventies. Benefits and costs are interdependent parts of a complex system. Forrester and Meadows struggled for about three decades to understand how it (the systems) works. Like their colleague System Thinkers all over the world they got a lot wiser overtime. Since the early birds Forrester and Meadows in 1971 started the discussion there has been a transformation in thinking & acting with systems from quick fix to wisdom that can be characterized by some elementary principles.

Thinking and acting wise[32]
- From reaction to co-creating;
- From symptoms to structures;
- From short notice to distant view;
- From me to we;

---

[30] Rein and Schon, Reframing policy discourse, eds. F. Fischer and J. Forrester, London UCL Press, 1993 p. 3
[31] J.W. Forrester, World Dynamics, Cambridge MA: Wright-Allen Press, 1971
[32] Systeemdenken, Bill Bryan, Michael Goodman, Jaap Schaveling, Academic Service, Sdu Uitgevers, Den Haag, p. 27

- From parts to the whole;
- From knowledge to learning;
- From knowing to developing.

Forrester and Meadows presented their totally new way of thinking in 1972 to an international group of businessmen, statesmen and scientists, known as the Club of Rome. The World was perplexed. The Club of Rome adopted the idea that what the World needs is much slower growth and in some cases no growth or negative growth.

In the decades that followed it soon turned out that in times of crisis there is not much attention for the environment. 'Zuerst kommt das Fressen, dan die Moral' German playwright Berthold Brecht stated[33] and history proves him right. In bad times we have to row the boat, although the three R's – Reuse, Reduce, Recycle - generally profit from crises. In good financial times however investments in new technologies and experimental innovation increase and people tend to be more generous towards other people they don't know.

Growth sec is not the problem. It is the quality of growth that counts. In order to show the difference we propose to replace the concept Growth by the broader concept Progress. For example sustainable development may be a fast growing sector. Although about 78% of all human activity is fuelled by digging up and burning the rotted remains of primeval swamps, according to Amory B. Lovins, 'we can move away from these fossil fuels by focusing on three simple principles: reduce use, modulate demand and optimize supply.'[34]

What happens here is nothing less than a change in the structure of systems. Such a change requires leverage. Leverage comes from new ways of thinking.

New Ways of Thinking include:
- Learning to see structures instead of events;
- Thinking in terms of change processes instead of in snap

---

[33] Dreigroschen Oper, Bertold Brecht, 1928, Food comes before moral sense.
[34] Reinventing Fire, bold business solutions for the new energy era, by Amory Lovins and Rocky Mountain Institute, Chelsea Green Publishing, 2011, p. 11

shots.[35]

'Once we see the relation between structure and behaviour, we can begin to understand how systems work,' Donella Meadows experienced.[36] She described a system as 'a set of things - people, cells, molecules, or whatever - interconnected in such a way that they produce their own pattern of behaviour over time'.

A system must consist of three kinds of things:
• Elements
• Interconnections
• A function or purpose

It is difficult to see through the behaviour of a system. One cannot detect it by fathoming the behaviour of the parts. The whole is more than the sum of the parts and, the conduct of the whole is not the same as the sum of behaviours of the parts. Meadows: 'You'll stop looking for who's to blame; instead you'll start asking, "What's the system?" The possibility of feedback opens up the idea that a system can cause its own behaviour.'

The reciprocity of things
Ever since the days of Jean Paul Sartre and Simone de Beauvoir the spirit of individualism fuelled emancipation movements. Women, workers, students, teenagers and minorities, they all fought for freedom and participation rights. Participation that involved consuming as well. Everybody wanted - and many still do - tickets to the fast growing material worlds of beverages, fast foods and nicotine. Coca Cola, McDonalds and Marlboro became major influencers of life styles, enabled to do so by canny communication and huge marketing budgets.

'The negative side of this "everybody get their own" exploitative attitude certainly is no longer appropriate,' Gary Snyder, American prizewinning poet and environmental activist, claimed.[37] 'It can be said to have been in

---

[35] A Systems Thinking Primer, Three Sigma, Inc. www.threesigma.com, Oct 20th 2009
[36] Donella Meadows, Thinking in Systems, Earthscan, 2001, page 1
[37] Gary Snyder, The Gary Snyder Reader, The 'East-West' Interview, Counterpoint Berkeley, 2000, p. 119

some ways productive when there were enormous quantities of resources available; but it is counterproductive in a post-frontier society. It's counter productive, since the important insight for everyone is how to interact appropriately and understand the reciprocity of things, which is the actual model of life on earth - a reciprocal, rather than a competitive, network.'[38]

As a matter of fact, Gary Snyder unveiled the spirit that leads to the answer of the central question of this book. Paraphrased the core question is: What can a person, a group, or a society, including the government, do to improve on the business as usual pattern, especially within the context of growing problems such as climate change, increasing income disparity and rising unemployment?

We are moving away from social Darwinism – the survival of the fittest - to ecological Darwinism: the survival of the most cooperative. Reasonable individuals who understand that cooperation, sharing and accumulative learning is in their own best interest put an end to competition. In an urgent situation like the one that is now rapidly unfolding, there is no room for fighting. We have entered a post-frontier society. Our main problems rise to a level that covers the people of all nations.

An unimaginable variety of options

Once one starts to think in systems the perceiving of the surroundings changes. The thinking becomes dynamic instead of static. 'A system that can evolve,' Meadows stated, 'can survive almost any change, by changing itself.'[39] A complex pattern can grow based on simple game rules. Meadows: 'The genetic code within the DNA that is the basis of all biological evolution contains just four different letters, combined into words of three letters each. That pattern, and the rules for replicating and rearranging it, has been constant for something like three billion years, during which it has spewed out an unimaginable variety of failed and successful self-evolved creatures.'[40]

---

[38] Gary Snyder, The Gary Snyder Reader, The 'East-West' Interview, Counterpoint Berkeley, 2000, p. 120
[39] Donella Meadows, Thinking in Systems, Earthscan, page 159
[40] Donella Meadows, Thinking in Systems, Earthscan, page 159/160

Donella Meadows' remark that one can only dance with systems implies that dancing scores better than talking. Meadows: 'There is a problem in discussing systems with words. Words and sentences must, by necessity come only one at a time in linear, logical order. Systems happen all at once. They are connected not just in one direction, but in many directions simultaneously.'

Forrester and Meadows pointed out that many people's knowledge is based on intuition instead of on measuring and fact-finding. The 17th century unflappable Dutch philosopher Baruch or Benedict Spinoza[41] already stated that intuition is the highest level of knowledge. Intuition scores higher than logic or reason: each answer (fact) leads to a following question (finding). Even measuring is not trustworthy most of the time. It is a very complex ability that starts with the problem of finding the right indicators whereupon the right model needs to be found. Neo-classical economists miss the bull's eye every time they try to predict the rise and fall of markets. This failure is due to the static models used and to the assumption that the future is a linear consequence of the past. In true life however this is never the case. Intuition, on the other hand, follows non-linear patterns. Intuition tells a person in a split second whether he/she likes another person or not. Intuition is the main house-seller that whispers in your ear 'this is your house' at the moment you enter for the first time. It is what Malcolm Gladwell described in Blink[42]: 'Whenever we meet someone for the first time, whenever we interview someone for a job, whenever we react to a new idea, whenever we're faced with making a decision quickly and under stress, we use that second part of our brain.' Gladwell means the so-called adaptive unconscious. A kind of giant computer that quickly and quietly processes a lot of the data we need in order to keep functioning as human beings.

An important distinction is between linear and non-linear thinking & acting. Linear thinkers start at step one and usually do a good and efficient job of completing the task before moving on to step two. They are driven, focused, and don't easily get off topic. Non-linear thinking is less constrictive - letting the creative side of themselves

---

[41] After he was excommunicated from the Jewish community in Amsterdam, 1656, Baruch Spinoza (1632-1677) changed his name into Benedict.
[42] Malcolm Gladwell, Blink, Back Bay Books, 2005, p.14

run rampant because of its' inherent lack of structure. It is very much like brainstorming - allowing thought to flow, unhindered, in attempts to arrive upon something special in the process.

It is important to have both types of thinkers on a team. Use non-linear thought to re-examine starting points and increase the possibility of finding the best option, and use linear thinkers and their efficient logic-based reasoning once a starting point has been established to get the job done in a timely manner.

It is the mixing of ideas, concepts, phases, instruments, linearity and non-linearity that generates 'meaning'.[43]

---

[43] C.J. Lofting, Patterns in Markets: the imposition of thinking patterns and the establishment of 'meaning' in trading systems. In distinguishing the basis for the two forms of analysis in the stock market, technical and fundamental, C. J. Lofting (Market Games: the 'what' and the 'where' in the stock market, 1999) focuses on a dichotomy that is equally relevant in the case of human values.

The Theory of Ecolution

Introduction

The question is how to organize society more sustainable, equal and fair? The conceptual framework, method and toolbox that were developed in *Only Winners* are of help. The matrix that is part of this method was briefly discussed in the paragraph 'The Force of the matrix'. The next chapter explains how to design and use a relevant matrix. This method including the seven criteria to select useful concepts was developed in the thesis Allemaal Winnen (Only Winners)[44].

The Ecolution Thinking Model shows a comprehensive graphic that summarizes a great deal of the thinking underneath the theory of ecolution. A society that values competition encourages the will to win. It has led to the contemporary state of resource depletion and deprivation (e.g. one billion extreme poor). This current social and ecological state is threatening the 'winners' as well, since the decrease of life-supporting systems will not stay confined within areas where the poor live. However much disagreement there may be, the majority of people seems convinced that the global ecological system does not comply with borders and laws. The most rational and optimal solution can be found in cooperation. Cooperation requires a completely different mindset from competition, e.g. different methods of decisionmaking and individuals who are able to share and learn accumulative.

Rising to higher potentialities

'We need a change,' Balder said. 'How?' a green feathery parrot posed the question. As a matter of fact 'How?' was the only question the parrot ever posed, so it came as no surprise to its' conversation partner. The man and the bird were the only customers of an open-air bar on the beach of Playa del Carmen, where swings had replaced the traditional barstools. Balder sat as quiet as he could, while the bird was moving to and fro with its' beak, as if he were the one on a swinging stool. 'Good question,' the man complimented the parrot. Then he

---

[44] Bakker & Van Empel, Allemaal Winnen, regionale duurzame ontwikkeling (Ecolutie), Erasmus University Rotterdam, NL, Studio nonfiXe, April 2012

picked up the bird and threw it in the air. 'Hey stupid, I can't fly. You cut my wings,' the parrot shrieked in panic. 'No I didn't, I just made you believe I did.' The parrot stretched its wings, a little feebly at first. It caught the wind, gained confidence and hovered away.

'The important thing is whether a person rises to his higher potentialities or falls away from them,' Balder called after the bird quoting a book he thought he'd forgotten about.[45]

'Everything in the world around us must be matched with some sense or power within us,' explained Schumacher, the economist who inspired Balder. 'Otherwise we remain unaware of its existence.' Why do some things happen and others do not? Change starts with awareness. We will not change patterns, habits and customs we are unaware off. We need to develop sensitivity for systems and relations. Next to the complexity of the systems that we are, we are part of, and that surround us[46], the global issues we face seem insolvable because of the opposites they incorporate. Controversies like justice and mercy add to the complexity. Awareness is needed to find answers as well as the result of the search for these answers. Like mercy and justice it is hard to combine freedom and order, yet a society needs both.

Before we can think of intervening, we have to transcend the issue, by stepping higher. Every schoolboy knows there is no freedom without some kind of order. At which point these two forces are in perfect balance, depends for example of the sense of responsibility of the individuals in the group and the group dynamics (or context). Responsibility overarches the other two faculties, bridges them and makes it possible to unite.

Ecolution leads to growing responsibility in the above case. (Brotherliness could have done the same job, but would lead to different strategies).

What we just did was part of Ecolution[47] thinking. To engage in one

---

[45] E.F. Schumacher, A Guide for the Perplexed, Harper Perennial 2004
[46] You and I are a system as well, just as our relationships with nature, with each other, with society in general.
[47] Ecolution: a. A natural development towards a system that is in balance - economic, ecologic and social; b. A continuous transition towards a higher level of economic, ecological and societal development; c. An expedition into the future, in

or more systems we need to develop awareness. Awareness perhaps is best described as a combination of knowledge, intuition and experience. Awareness can lead us to the higher level that bridges the dilemma by transcending, as we have seen responsibility overarching the dilemma between freedom and order. In turn the experience of transcending to such a higher level can lead to growing awareness.

Here we enter the heart of the matrix. The tasks of the ecolution matrix are: 1) to give meaning to a development within a specific context; 2) to show successes and failures; 3) to enable strategy design for a sustainable future.
The concept we chose was awareness. In the case of the parrot, quite a simple matrix evolved, in which Balders' act to throw the bird in the air was the performance of ecolution in all three solutionfinding clusters:

Phase/Solution Finding Cluster	Destruction	Deconstruction	Construction
Behaviour	Not flying parrot		Power within
Technology/Institutionalization	Cutting wings		Grown wings
Decisionmaking	Balder decides for the bird		The bird decides for itself

For a society that needs freedom ánd order, an awareness level like the parrot reached at the construction phase will be fertile soil. The bird behaved with a power from within, the air column supported its wings that had been allowed to grow and the animal acted out of free will. The parrot is on the verge of reaching awareness (in a story animals can become aware, even self-aware). When freedom and order are put

---

search of behaviour, technology / institutionalization and governance that ensure a livable planet.
Ecolution is not confined within a strict frame or definition on purpose, but it holds some important elements:
  • The three capitals – economy, ecology and society – are equivalent;
  • Every society, community, organization, group or individual can apply ecolution;
  • Change is perpetual, always and everywhere;
  • The goal is continuous progress towards another level.

together, something starts to itch. We sense tension and anxiety while trying to unite the concepts. We are aware of the inner conflict of the opposites. For reconciliation we need to climb to a higher level. What can possibly reconcile these opposites? To be able to rise to the higher level in matrix-terms we need a three-dimensional figure, a kind of tower, of which the above matrix is the groundfloor. The first floor can be entered through a higher level of awareness. Almost like playing a video game: Plus One for Awareness gives access to a new playing field.

The dilemma can be solved by 'responsibility'. To reach such a solution concepts like the 'harm-principle' John Stuart Mill speaks of in On Liberty are supportive. A person is free to the extent that he or she harms no other, then the state can interfere. This is a political, and sometimes even religious, point of view. A community has to agree on it. Another perspective can be: People are selfish and deceitful, therefore strict hierarchy (operational excellence) and control are needed to keep the community from evolving into chaos. Now responsibility is replaced by strict hierarchy and control, which leads to a completely different society.

The latter however cannot be defined as ecolution. It is not aiming at a higher ecological, economic, social and psychological level. The social and psychological elements fall from their potentials.

Now we can design a matrix for a development that leads to a society with a sound mix of freedom and order.

Phase/Solution Finding Cluster	Destruction	Deconstruction	Construction
Behaviour	Selfish		Social
Technology/Institutionalization	Control mechanisms		Trust and Transparency
Decisionmaking	Top down		Bottom up

From this point forwards the crucial questions are:
- How can selfish people become social people?
- How can control be transformed into trust?

- Why do organizations have to reorganize complex structures and decisionmaking procedures?

Can we find a one-concept-fixes-all answer for these three questions? Yes, we can: JES! In a Joint Effort Society people behave socially by definition. The dominant culture is based on trust. Initiatives bubble up from deep down under. This leads to the question: How do we realize JES? Manfred Max-Neef and Fritz Schumacher provided inspiration.

Max-Neef stated that empowering the civil society fertilizes the soil for Human Scale Development, a JES-like concept. 'This is not to minimize the importance of the state, but to develop further the potential role of social actors, of social participation and of local communities.'[48]

Schumacher put much emphasis on education, decentralization and entrepreneurship. Entrepreneurs are the kind that suddenly have an idea or see an opportunity and off they go with the future of a whole community on their back. 'All history,' he wrote, 'as well as current experience, points to the fact that it is man, not nature, who provides the primary resource, that the key factor of all economic development comes out of the mind of man. Suddenly, there is an outburst of daring, initiative, invention, constructive activity, not in one field alone, but in many fields all at once. No one may be able to say where it came from in the first place; but we can see how it maintains and even strengthens itself: through various kinds of schools, in other words, through education'.[49]

Adding concepts to the context[50]

Opposites not only attract, they also distract, they stir curiosity, they tickle enthusiasm and particularly they create dynamics. By using opposite concepts a rather dull discourse can be changed into a revolutionary manifesto overnight. The Austrian/American economist

---

[48] Manfred A. Max-Neef, Human Scale Development, The Apex Press, New York, 1992, p.198

[49] E.F. Schumacher, Small is Beautiful, Harper & Row Publishers, New York, 1973, p. 83,84

[50] Based on Allemaal Winnen, Bakker & Van Empel, Jacques Derrida and E.F. Schumacher.

Joseph Schumpeter put two contradicting concepts in one explosive idea: Creative Destruction. It is a concept that has the power to blow up every status quo. Creative Destruction has a lot in common with Jacques Derrida's 'Deconstruction'. Derrida claimed that human thinking is based on opposites. By turning these opposites around and upside down, by permitting disorder and chaos, he provoked paradigm shifts. Derrida believed in change. For that reason he promoted disorganizing existing concepts and terms and the design of new different frameworks and cadres. Along these lines he proposed to restructure the human brain, so it can let go of old paradigms and create new ones.

Deconstruction

Developments tend to erode at some point and turn from positive into negative. That point more than often is reached as soon as people stop to ask questions and take a situation or institution for granted, i.e. stop reframing. When dogmas say 'Hello', one could say, sustainable development says 'Goodbye'! For example the Industrial Revolution that started in the beginning of last century brought many positive changes, like growing prosperity, better healthcare, higher educational levels and rising employability.

Today we suffer from other consequences, such as climate change, exhausted resources and growing inequality. The Industrial Revolution turned from being constructive into destructive. Jacques Derrida taught that deconstruction is an expedition to the source in order to find new ways into the future[51]. Deconstruction can be defined as purposely disordering existing systems to create space for innovation on human scale. Change is inevitable. It is the dynamic that creates life. The species that will survive is the species that can adapt to change[52]. Agility and flexibility of the human race decide whether humans will inhabit the Earth in the future or not. Deconstruction is one of the ways to deal with change and to turn worn-out systems, structures, policies and destructive behaviour, technology and decisionmaking into productive, healthy and livable life-styles.

---

[51] Erik Oger, Derrida, een Inleiding, 2006
[52] Charles Darwin, The origin of species, 1872, translated in Dutch by Ludo Hellemans, 2001, Uitgeverij Nieuwezijds

Filling the matrix with concept triads

The dialectic method of thesis, antithesis and synthesis forces the mind to come up with relevant concepts[53] for the issue at stake without previous valuation. Thinking in opposites (thesis - antithesis) and then looking for the synthesis, offers clear insights in 'how things work' and 'where to go from here'. In the theory of ecolution the dichotomies are related to developments that can be considered beneficial or harmful for a sustainable development. As we have seen, there are two sorts of problems: those that can be killed by logical thinking (the invention of the car, of the refrigerator, the washing machine, etcetera) and those that cannot be solved, because they incorporate inner opposites, like freedom and order.

The distinction between order and freedom is a basic one. Many further pairs of opposites have a strong resemblance. Centralization for instance has to do with order. Decentralization with freedom. Order is associated with efficiency. Freedom calls for intuition and leads to innovation. The larger an organization is, the stronger the call for order. But if that means that there is no room for creative intuition and entrepreneurial disorder it becomes a moribund organization. Schumacher stated: 'In any organization, large or small, there must be a certain clarity and orderliness; if things fall into disorder, nothing can be accomplished. Yet orderliness, as such is static and lifeless; so there also must be plenty of elbowroom and scope for breaking through the established order, to do the thing never done before, never anticipated by the guardians of orderliness the new unpredicted and unpredictable outcome of a man's creative idea. Therefore any organization has to strive continuously for the orderliness of order and the disorderliness of creative freedom.'[54] The heart of the matrix is a continuous struggle between opposites. It creates the dynamics and tension that generate energy. Whether the outcomes are positive or negative differs from one situation to the other. What the development will be depends on the power of the

---

[53] A concept can be defined as the mental representation of an abstract, general idea, or of the cluster of related ideas. Concepts support the communication of complex ligatures.

[54] E.F. Schumacher, Small is Beautiful, Economics as if People Mattered, p. 259, 260

used concepts. Which ones are useful and productive and which aren't cannot be said in advance. Exploration, experiment and watchfulness are needed.

The matrix is a passage through time, that starts from a withered, depressing state of destruction and ends in a promising or already blossoming state of construction. In between both anti-poles we'll trace a black box where the metamorphosis takes place. Nobody knows exactly how it happens. A society is a multi-knot network where everything happens at once. It is too complex to understand, logically. Each concept is a piece of the puzzle that is our reality, although it is a single linear part of the complex nonlinear whole. By bringing more concepts for all three solutionfinding clusters into the matrix we come to understand how things might be related. It is a model that comes as close as possible to reality, because it shows relationships and connections. At the same time, thinking about solutions in terms of concepts raises awareness, inspires people and organizations to change their behaviour, to develop new technologies, or decide in a different way. This type of thinking encourages the reconciliation of opposites and supports the quest for a higher level of awareness.

Mental framework
'Remember, always, that everything you know, and everything everyone knows, is only a model. Get your model out there where it can be. Invite others to challenge your assumptions and add their own ... nothing more than practicing the scientific method - something that is done too seldom, even in science, and is done hardly at all in social science or management or government or everyday life.'
Donella H. Meadows

Apart from the reciprocity of systems that is not in most economists' models, the linearity of the models doesn't comply with reality. In real life nothing, apart from human constructs such as highways and canals, is a straight line. Nature and other systems consist of circuits, cycles, rhizomes, spirals, anything but a straight line from a to b. The things that happen and the other things that do not happen, are the outcome of the operations of this nonlinear complexity of systems. Change in one system, causes changes in all others and does so perpetually, and thereby leads to unforeseen changes.

The Theory of Ecolution is an attempt to support individuals and the communities they form to actively explore life together with others in a generous way. Nature is generous and wild. The home of mankind floating in boundless space is a generous house providing for all needs, circulating life. It is renewing life over and over, amending, adapting and improving. Man taps into this system, creates and destroys, exerts strenuous efforts to overcome entropy and death. The strategy however, has to change. For the systems we built within the system are been proven to be destructive.

Ecolution is concerned with the spiritual, psychological, economic and ecological adaptation of mankind to changing circumstances, rather than the physical and genetic adaptation of mankind. Psychiatrist and writer Erich Fromm, impressed by research on behalf of the Club of Rome (1973), already stressed the urgency to adapt human behaviour. Fromm: 'A profound change of mentality is necessary in order to prevent an economic and ecological catastrophe.'[55]

Erich Fromm noticed that the Club of Rome represented the spectrum featured by quantification, abstract and depersonification, a thing he found remarkable given the conclusions. Conclusions that he shared with radical humanist and economist E.F. Schumacher: 'For the first time in history the physical survival of mankind depends on a profound change in human mentality. A change in human mentality however is only possible, when drastic economic and social changes offer men and women the opportunity to change their attitude and give the courage and vision to succeed in changing mentality.'[56]

---

[55] Erich Fromm, Een kwestie van hebben of zijn, grondslagen voor een nieuwe levensoriëntatie in de consumptiemaatschappij, Bijleveld, Utrecht, 3e druk 1987. Original title To Have or To Be? p 18
[56] Erich Fromm, Een kwestie van hebben of zijn, grondslagen voor een nieuwe levensoriëntatie in de consumptiemaatschappij, Bijleveld, Utrecht, 3e druk 1987. Original title To Have or To Be? p. 19

Ecolution Thinking Model

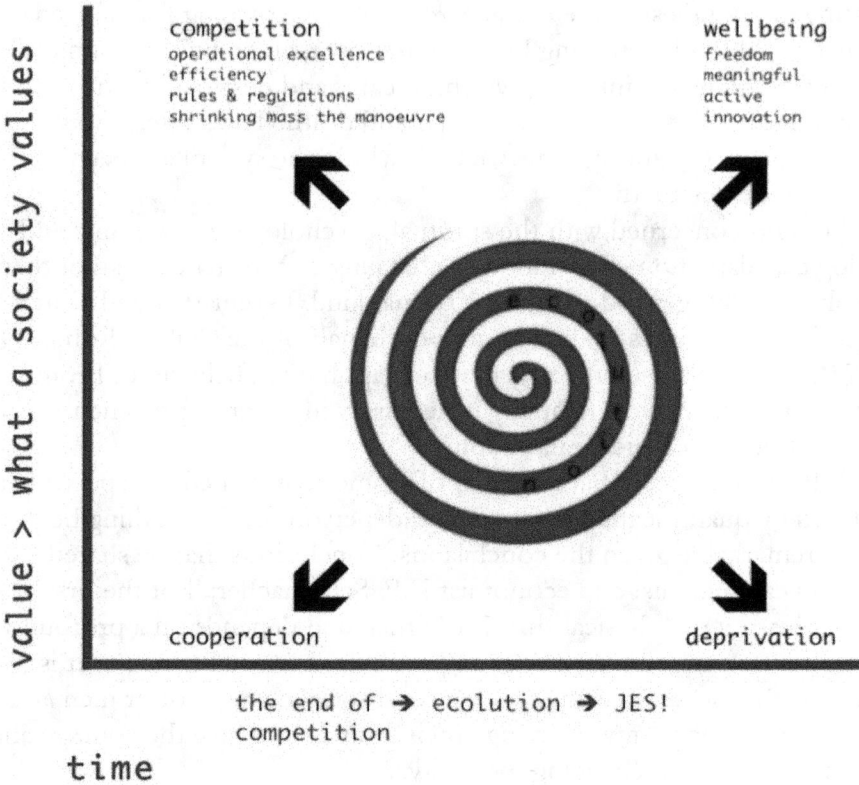

competition
operational excellence
efficiency
rules & regulations
shrinking mass the manoeuvre

wellbeing
freedom
meaningful
active
innovation

cooperation

deprivation

the end of → ecolution → JES!
competition

value > what a society values

time

Legenda: A society that values competition chooses for operational excellence, efficiency, and rules and regulations that lead to shrinking mass the manoeuvre of the individual, deprivation and resource depletion. The society that values cooperation is based on sharing and accumulative learning. Freedoms and innovation encourage active and productive citizenship, leading to meaningful wellbeing for the individual. Ecolution puts an end to the era of competition. This dynamic movement resets developments and creates awareness. It has to be applied before slack enters the system. This way a society can continuously reach for a higher ecological, economic, socio-cultural and psychological level.

The ecolution thinking model shows how destruction can be turned into construction, and also that the trend is already in motion. More than ever, it is visible how developments in one corner of the world affect other parts, other people and, other markets. This system of systems shows the interconnection of all with everything and changes speed the globe.

We are the enemy
Ideas that underlie the End of Competition[57]:
1. Competition gives birth to winners and losers. Winners add value. Losers distract value. All in all this may very well be a zero sum game for society. Business and society at large are better of once competition oriented companies become cooperative and put their money on the innovation card, trying to find a solution nobody has mentioned yet;
2. People start to work together when there is a mutual enemy or crisis, and urgency is felt. Here the Enemy = Us. We - mankind - are our own enemy. 'What can I do?' is a logical question. Every individual has to answer this question personally, and will find out that all answers are different.

For a long time the predominant adage has been: competition stirs innovation. But even in a competitive environment, parties work together to achieve a mutual goal, beat the mutual enemy. When this enemy becomes a global thing, people and organizations are better off when they work together, co-create, share and cooperate.
This cooperation and sharing will be a mix of both contradictory characteristics of people - selfishness and altruism - that can be defined as Self Interest. It will be out of Self Interest that man decides greed is not enough and will start Joint Efforts.

The European Union is a good example of a natural development rooted in a simple insight: countries are better off when they work together than when at war with each other. Already in the mid nineteenth century philosophers, writers and artists dreamed of a 'United States of Europe', as Victor Hugo expressed in his speech Fraternity is my Revenge in 1849. We will return to Hugo's words in

---

[57] These two insights are the results of observation, analysis and in-depth desk research.

the paragraph The concept of brotherhood.

Cooperating, sharing and learning seem far away from the capitalist model that has been dominant in the world of economics for centuries. The capitalist mentality is competitive: Winner takes all. A recent study on social and cognitive processes that underlie human cumulative culture[58] compared the behaviour of children, chimpanzees and capuchin monkeys. The research revealed that the cooperative capacity of people allows them to solve problems one person (or ape) cannot solve alone. The children shared information and taught each other how to overcome obstacles. The apes did not. Moreover the children tolerated that another kid got the bonus. They intuitively knew this would improve the teamwork and therefore increase the chance to gain the bigger, even more desirable, price that lay ahead after the next challenge.

This capacity for cooperation, which has to do with behaviour and ways of decisionmaking, is just what we need to reach the construction phase after the past shambolic years of crises on almost every societal, political, ecological and economic terrain that deconstructed and upset many systems. The transformation towards cooperation is already visible in different places on different scales in society.

Selecting concepts
One of the basic thoughts underneath JES! and the theory of ecolution, is that the complexity of reality and continuous changing circumstances cannot be captured in a static model. However, we do need a model and we do need to compartmentalize reality to be able to sketch it and find the lever points for change. Therefore, the theory of ecolution comes up with a dynamic model that visualizes plans for action (concepts). Some concepts are derived from theories of scholars, others are fruits of observation, analyses and imagination. All concepts are compressed into words that show a development from a state of destruction, through the black box of deconstruction towards a state of construction.

The matrix is a model that shows how concepts evolve through phases

---

[58] Identification of the Social and Cognitive Processes Underlying Human Cumulative Culture, by L. G. Dean, R. L. Kendal, S. J. Schapiro, B. Thierry, K. N. Laland, Science 335, 1114 (2012)

(destruction, deconstruction, construction). A person, a group, organization or community that designs a strategy for the future, has to think of relevant concepts to be able to move the solutionfinding clusters, behaviour, technology / institutionalization and decisionmaking, into the construction phase. The theory of ecolution deliberately leaves the choice of concepts open. Two arguments for this flexibility are:

1. In time and in different societies other concepts can be thought of as valuable;
2. New concepts will be discovered.

The purpose is to leave as much space as possible for freedom, diversity and change while striving for a joint effort society. Such a society inherently opposes plans for action that are destructive for people or the planet. We rule out such concepts by proposing seven selection criteria. Acts, innovations, thoughts, forms of governing that do not comply with these, do not belong in the ecolution matrix.

Seven criteria for concepts:[59]

1. A concept has to contribute to human wellbeing in the broad sense of the word. It should stimulate integral economic, ecological, energetic, psychological and social-cultural upgrading of (a certain) society and may not harm one or more of these elements;
2. A concept helps to ensure that natural resources like clean water, fresh air and fertile soil may only be used if nature can reproduce them in a sustainable manner;
3. A concept should inspire people, companies, institutes and governments to change their behaviour, in order to catalyze and support a more sustainable societal development of balances and synergies among Profit, Planet and People;
4. A concept needs to be validated and recommended by those involved;
5. A concept should stimulate open and honest dialogue, which should lead to sharing of knowledge, skills and experiences that make it possible to work together as equals.

---

[59] Numbers 6 and 7 originate from the Natural Step Framework, a comprehensive model for planning in complex systems.

6. A concept should contribute to the elimination of our (a community's) contribution to the progressive buildup of substances extracted from the Earth's crust (for example heavy metals and by-products of fossil fuels) and or chemicals and compounds produced by society (for example dioxins, PCBs and DDT);
7. A concept should contribute to the elimination of our (a community's) contribution to the progressive physical degradation and destruction of nature and natural processes (for example over-harvesting forests and paving over critical wildlife habitats and should not result in conditions that undermine people's capacity to meet their basic human needs, for example unsafe working conditions and inadequate salaries.

In practice the change will not be easy because of inwardly focused cultures, paralyzing bureaucracies, parochial politics, a low level of trust, lack of teamwork, arrogant attitudes, greed, dysfunctional leadership, or the general human fear of the unknown.[60] Whatever the reason may be the ecolution matrix has to deal with it, or show alternative approaches.

Every change process here is reduced to triads. Each triad is part of one of these three clusters of instruments (the toolkit for solving problems and tackling issues):

1. A change in the behaviour of people and organizations;
2. Technological progress, design driven innovation and/or institutional solutions;
3. (Alternative) methods of decisionmaking.

These solutionfinding clusters originate from the field research done on behalf of Only Winners[61]. They cover all society's movements and are the wheels to turn for fundamental change comprising individual actions, governance and the technological and institutional innovations that can support or obstruct behaviour and/or governance fashions.

---

[60] John P. Kotter, Leading Change, Harvard Business School Press 1996, p 20.
[61] Allemaal Winnen, regionale duurzame ontwikkeling (Ecolutie), Bakker & Van Empel, Erasmus University, Studio nonfiXe, April, 2012

Stories we can tell

Every combination along the horizontal and vertical axes of the matrix is part of the storyline. In order to get a compelling story, the storyteller has to draw lines among the 3 x 3 = 9 'knots' to reveal the relations. Stories put flesh and blood to the bones. They are among the oldest of methods to educate as well as to create cohesion in a group. A shared story is like powerful glue. Children are brought up with fairytales and family chronicles to teach them where they come from, what ethics to live by and to stir the imagination that is needed to deal with the tough things in life. Religions use stories to keep the faithful from wandering away from the herd. Companies use stories to sell their products. Organizations motivate their employees by creating a gesamt story. The population of a country shares a history that is taught in schools. One of the features of literature is that it improves understanding.

People love to tell and to hear stories. In order to put the matrix with concepts to work, we translate the singular words back to a story, the compelling story of our future.

The matrix is also a kind of barometer. It gives an indication: do things look good or bad? It doesn't make sense to sketch detailed forecasts, definitely not for the long run. Predictions tend to outlive themselves. But we can develop a sense for the direction developments are taking and use the matrix as an orientation tool. Is this development stimulating constructive behaviour, or not? Does this technology add value or does it lead to environmental problems? Do we need these regulations or are they excluding people? Do we agree with the paramilitary force our president calls for, or is this a step in the direction of dictatorship?

The added value of the matrix is that complex, reciprocal and interrelated factors can be presented in one framework. The matrix distinguishes nine ways to look at an issue or problem. Every action to solve the problem or clear the issue can be assigned to one of the dimensions. The matrix also shows the implications that a certain action can have regarding the two other dimensions. This quality makes it possible to develop in a sustainable way and include the wellbeing of individual people in measuring today and acting for tomorrow.

There is not a one and only Matrix with a capital M. Each person, each organization can make their own, together with all those involved.[62] This is exploration and experimentation at the same time. To fill a matrix with relevant concepts the stakeholders need to decide together what is the issue for which they are searching a solution and how they proceed in finding the answer or answers. This is process is evidence of practicing decisionmaking. Thus concepts for decisionmaking are explored and tried while filling a matrix. The same goes for the other clusters; selecting concepts is the first step in trying them.

Exploring coffee machine issues

Some issues rise like a mountain in front of the eye, others are obvious for square thinkers and keen observers. Some come to light through scientific research, but there are also the coffee machine issues. These are invisible to the naked eye, but decisive in the functioning of a system. Often each involved person holds a part of the issue but isn't aware of this. If you ask them they will tell you honestly they know nothing. However as soon as they meet at the coffee corner of the office valuable management information about the wellbeing of the organization is shared. The type of information the manager never hears and that is not being discussed at meetings. There are a few methods to explore the coffee machine issues. We highlight two options.[63]

1. Fly on the wall

This involves independent writers who join meetings and use novel techniques to describe what goes on in a group or an organization. The writer listens to what is being said, but even more to the things that aren't said; silences, body-language, rumours in hallways and at coffee stands. The writer does not intervene in the process between the actors. He or she observes while staying almost invisible, like a fly on the wall. A fly is free to follow hearsay, intuition or announcements. Then she or he certainly registers whatever turbulence there may be in the formal and informal structures of the organization. All thus

---

[62] Selection criteria for concepts 4 & 5. 4. A concept needs to be validated and recommended by those involved; 5. A concept should stimulate open and honest dialogue, which should lead to sharing of knowledge and experiences that make it possible to work together as equals.
[63] The Fly on the Wall and In the Bus methods have been used by the authors in culture change programmes at Essent and Enexis, energy companies in the Netherlands, 2004 – 2008.

gathered information is written down in an exciting story. It probably contains the unconscious motives, observed attitudes, hypotheses about how to interpret gossip and rumours, sketches of the movers and followers in discussions.

An important question is, to whom does the fly report? It is also essential to emphasize that s/he should not be biased, but should be at the service of the whole! Authorisation of the story by the people involved is necessary. They will have to recognize themselves and the way things are done in the story. This method is flexible, dynamic, unveiling, often surprising, cleansing, clearing and above all constructive;

2. In the Bus

The essence of this method is to talk to people outside their working habitat, in an environment that makes them comfortable as well as open. For instance: Use an old Volkswagen camper bus. One you can sit in with at least four people, around a table. Pick up your guest at home early in the morning, make sure he or she feels comfortable and drive the bus into the country, to a place that appeals to the guests' imagination. Cater your guest with some delicious food and drinks, put on easy listening music. Then talk about whatever comes to mind, listen carefully, hear what is not being said and you will find out what motivates the person you are interviewing. You will also get a deeper insight into how an organization or network functions. Last but not least, bring the guest in time to his or her office. Write their portrait using novel techniques and ask for authorization before sending it to his or her manager or before publishing it.

The Fly and the Bus can be complementary. They add value to the matrix, because the story outputs can shine a light on the organization and the people in it. Relevant concepts can be derived to make a change and a strategy can be unfolded.

Measuring quality

'What we measure affects what we do; and if our measurements are flawed, decisions may be distorted'[64], Stiglitz, Sen and Fitoussi wrote

---

[64] Mis-measuring our lives, Why GDP doesn't add up, Joseph E. Stiglitz, Amartya Sen and Jean-Paul Fitoussi, the report by the commission on the measurement of economic

in Mis-measuring our lives. These three economists headed the commission on the measurement of economic performance and social progress installed by the French president Nicolas Sarkozy in 2008. The commission wished to establish 'a broad statistical system that captures as many of the relevant dimensions as possible'. The current measuring system (of Gross Domestic Product or GDP) doesn't match people's perceptions and nibbles away the legitimacy of politics. Next to this, policy and decisions based on wrong information lead to undesired outcomes. GDP not only doesn't measure wellbeing, neither does it capture sustainability. Wellbeing has to do with economic resources such as income and wealth - on household level - but with other aspects of people's lives as well: what they do, what they can do, how they feel and the natural environment they live in. These sentences refer to the Capability Approach of Amartya Sen and Martha Nussbaum that puts the opportunity 'to live the life one has reason to value' on top of all societal efforts. It appeared a sign for improvement that the right wing president of France, Nicolas Sarkozy, installed a commission headed by unconventional economists such as Sen and Stiglitz to research the evaluating measurements of conventional economic politics. The emphasis was redirected to wellbeing instead of wealth.

Wellbeing has to do with the quality of life and how people perceive changes in the quality of their lives.

Capturing quality of life, and the changing levels of this quality in indicators is an enormous challenge. The authors of Mis-measuring our lives developed twelve recommendations – or principles - on how to perform such an attempt[65] :

1. When evaluating material wellbeing, look at income and consumption rather than production;
2. Emphasize the household perspective;
3. Consider income and consumption jointly with wealth;
4. Give more prominence to the distribution of income, consumption and wealth;

performance and social progress, The New Press, 2010, p. 2

[65] Mis-measuring our lives, Why GDP doesn't add up, Joseph E. Stiglitz, Amartya Sen and Jean-Paul Fitoussi, the report by the commission on the measurement of economic performance and social progress, The New Press, 2010.

5. Broaden income measures to non-market activities. Here the commission referred to home-produced consumption – such as growing own food – but to leisure as well;
6. Quality of life depends on people's objective conditions and capabilities. Steps should be taken to improve measures of people's health, education, personal activities and environmental conditions. In particular, substantial effort should be devoted to developing and implementing robust, reliable measures of social connections, political voice and insecurity that can be shown to predict life satisfaction;
7. Quality-of-life indicators in all the dimensions covered should assess inequalities in a comprehensive way;
8. Surveys should be designed to assess the links between various quality-of-life domains for each person, and this information should be used when designing policies in various fields;
9. Statistical offices should provide the information needed to aggregate across quality-of-life dimensions, allowing the construction of different indices;
10. Measures of both objective and subjective wellbeing provide key information about people's quality of live. Statistical offices should incorporate questions to capture people's life- evaluations, hedonic experiences and priorities in their own survey;
11. Sustainability assessment requires a well-identified dashboard of indicators. The distinctive feature of the components of this dashboard should be that they are interpretable as variations of some underlying 'stocks'. A monetary index of sustainability has its place in such a dashboard but, under the current state of the art, it should remain essentially focused on economic aspects of sustainability;
12. The environmental aspects of sustainability deserve a separate follow-up based on a well-chosen set of physical indicators. In particular there is a need for a clear indicator of our proximity to dangerous levels of environmental damage (such as associated with climate change or the depletion of fishing stocks)

Wellbeing has some quantitative features that can be used to deduce information - such as household income, consumption and wealth, crime statistics, childbirth and death numbers, live-expectancy, literacy, et cetera. Next to these objective factors that we need to examine carefully in order not to misinterpret them or use the wrong information, subjective wellbeing, changing levels and future strategies and policies must be researched.

Further on you will find more attempts to redirect economic policy evaluations away from GDP that is increasingly perceived as one-dimensional and disfunctional. These approaches fit into the process of growing awareness on what economics should be and should do. A paradigm shift on values that puts cooperation instead of competition at the heart of our valuation system is necessary to be able to re-design society. However the ongoing financial crisis, since December 2007, evoked fear and in practice politics has not been coming up with any policy that improves the wellbeing of people. Nicolas Sarkozy, the enlightened French president that commissioned Mis-measuring our lives, showed himself a utterly conservative with matching economic views during the elections in France, four years after the release of the report. Over the whole, from 2008 to 2012 contraction and large cuts in government spending on education, healthcare and the arts, have been showing a turn around, back to neo-classical axioms, back to a winner-takes-all mentality that dominated the 1980's under the banners of Margaret Thatcher and Ronald Reagan.

A politician who passionately defended some of the principles that characterize a joint effort society is Glenda Jackson, MP in the British House of Commons, on April 10, 2013. The occasion was the tribute to the late Margaret Thatcher. After a lively description of the deprivation many, many British fell into, the growing amount of homeless, the deplorable state schools and hospitals were in during the Thatcher era, Mrs. Jackson said: 'What concerns me is that I am beginning to see what might be the re-emergence of that total traducing of what I regard as the spiritual basis of this country where we do care about society, where we do believe in communities, where we do not leave people and walk by on the other side. That is not happening now, but if we go back to the heyday of that era, I fear that we will see replicated yet again the extraordinary human damage from which we as a nation have suffered and the talent that has been totally wasted because of the inability genuinely to see the individual value of every single human being.'[66]

The individual value of every single human being, his or her opportunities to live the life they have reason to value, to do what they can, be who they are, that is the essence of the joint effort society. Margaret Thatcher was inspired by Friedrich von Hayek, whose 'Road to Serfdom' is said to have left a permanent mark on her political character.[67] Von Hayek was a fervent promoter of neo-liberal economics. He thought it a governmental task to install measures that guarantee competition to do its' works, regardless the social and ecological costs.[68]

Fresh school agreement

Returning from the French internal political affairs and the British House of Commons where Thatcher's legacy was discussed to the edge, we focus again on methods of deciding what concepts are relevant to certain situations and how to find these.

Through the Fly, the Bus, Method Holistic Participation[69] (or other consultation approaches) the people involved can determine their shared vision on the issue at stake. For example: We want healthy and smart kids and the school is the place where they get educated. Research by a health organization showed that the indoor climate in Dutch schools often was unhealthy and affected the learning achievements of pupils. The regional government of the province Noord-Brabant set up a Method Holistic Participation session. Parents, teachers, school management and government officials agreed on creating a healthier indoor climate for a particular school that

---

[66] Glenda Jackson, MP UK, Tributes to Baroness Thatcher at the House of Commons, April 10, 2013

[67] Edward Milliband, MP UK, Tributes to Baroness Thatcher at the House of Commons, April 10, 2013

[68] Economics Unmasked, from power and greed to compassion and the common good, Philip B. Smith & Manfred Max-Neef, Green Books, 2012

[69] The Method Holistic Participation was designed by Peter Schmid. He combined the insights on teamwork in construction of Gropius and Wachsmann with kindred-spirited team-processes that, as he had found out, already occurred in ancient clans and cultures. All involved the approach of an issue from different angles. Schmid's method focuses on developing solutions by all involved and includes participating experts. Ecological and participation problems that need to be solved are incorporated in the MHP. The MHP is based on systematic teamwork and consensus building, and it's down to earth.

needed to be refurbished.

The group started to look for information, exchange experience, visit best practices on the issue and accumulate knowledge. Then they discussed relevant concepts, such as nontoxic materials, fresh air inside classrooms, the school building as a living and breathing organism et cetera. One of the teachers suggested an eco-literacy curriculum for the pupils. The budget however was limited. A commission was put to work to concretize the concepts. The first action was stocktaking: what do we have, what do we need, how can we pay for it? The commission followed the guidelines set up by the stakeholders and consulted with experts on natural building.

The fresh air concept made them investigate different ventilation systems, some of them very advanced. The price tag on such systems turned out quite high. Next to the purchase price a considerable budget was needed to maintain the system. At one of the expert meetings, an architect on natural building stood up in the middle of the discussion on which system would be most suitable. He walked to the window and opened it. 'Here is your ventilation system,' he said. 'It is all about behaviour. Teachers and children have to become aware of the suffocating atmosphere in the room and open the windows.' 'You can do that in summertime, but when it freezes, the classroom will be too cold,' someone replied. 'Yes, and draughty.' 'The noises from outside will distract the children,' others added. The architect walked to the whiteboard and drew a room with windows arranged in a certain way. 'If you place the windows right there will be no draught,' he explained. 'The kids have a break every hour,' one of the teachers added. 'During this break we can air the classroom.'

The solution was found in a combination of technology and behaviour and the windows were designed in such a manner that opening them wouldn't cause draught. Plus the issue was incorporated in the eco-literacy program; raising awareness and educating children and teachers to air the room during breaks.

Measuring the matrix
A Matrix filled with concepts asks for positioning by the people involved - the stakeholders. Where do they place a concept; in which

phase can the development be placed for each of the three solutionfinding clusters?

To understand how a group of people feels about a development, a survey asking them to give grades on a scale of 1 to 5 (very bad – bad – in transition – good – excellent) can be illuminating.

The purpose of ecolution is to trace development processes and to design a strategy and a method that moves the whole process forward to a higher economic, ecological and social level.

The matrix shows an overview on how people feel about a development; if they think it can lead to progress and supports them in what they do, what they can do, how they feel, and improve the natural environment in which they live. The matrix can create awareness on systems and how to create change (behaviour, technology/institutionalization, decisionmaking). And the matrix can support a shared vision of the future.

To find out what people do, think and feel, which concepts are relevant for them and how they perceive developments, one can perform a study such as the health organization did in the fresh school example. And survey later. Or start with a survey and evaluate again. But whatever method you use, try to make sure that everybody involved is engaged. Success or failure depends for a large part on the involvement of people. It is a bottom-up thing, not top down. Hierarchies don't achieve ecolution. Top down commands are in the destruction phase of the decisionmaking cluster, they lead to apathy, disobedience, go at the cost of participation and freedom. The process of choosing concepts and filling the matrix creates awareness at the same time.

Likert scale

The so-called 'Likert scale' named after its' inventor, psychologist Rensis Likert, is a five point scale.[70] A good Likert scale balances on both sides of a neutral option. It is a method to measure subjective information such as personal opinions, knowledge, abilities, and attitudes. Likert questions enable to create surveys that evaluate the intensity of respondents' feelings towards statements presented to

---

[70] Likert scale, Web Center for Social Research Methods

them. For classification one or more of seven measurement scales can be used:

1. One to Five (1 – 5)
2. One to Eight (1 – 8)
3. Agreement scale (disagree – agree)
4. Satisfaction scale (dissatisfied – satisfied)
5. Frequency scale (never – always)
6. Importance scale (unimportant – important)
7. Opposition scale (oppose – support)

The scores are summed up or their mean is calculated to give a rough indication of the searched for information. The numbers have to be interpreted. In fact each number represents a certain range:

1 = 0 – 20%
2 = 20 – 40%
3 = 40 – 60%
4 = 60 – 80%
5 = 80 – 100%

The outcomes are not absolute. Everything is relative. We know that 'strongly agree' is a lower score than 'agree', but we do not know how much lower it is. That is why we cannot make the mathematical calculations economists prefer. However for the purpose of policy- and decisionmaking, evaluating people's opinions and behaviour etc. it will do.

Plans for action

Introduction
The theory of ecolution approaches reality as a jungle of intertwined, interconnected and reciprocal systems that together form a rhizome and that is perceived different by every person depending on her or his situation, experiences, expectations, cultural and historical background, structural and political framework, knowledge, awareness, beliefs and fears.

To understand what is going on people need to know the context in which events occur and have to become aware of their own and the other's frameworks and paradigms that determine their view on the world surrounding them. Then they can change. They deconstruct paradigms and the systems that are built upon those worldviews. Deconstruction makes room for creation so behaviour, decisionmaking and technology and institutionalization can be turned to the direction of construction.

The architectural approach Bernard Tschumi introduced combined the context with concepts to give meaning (content) to a building in its' surroundings. The theory of ecolution operates similar to that approach. In the following paragraphs concepts, plans for action, to lift societal, ecological and individual wellbeing are discussed.

These are concepts that stimulate or harm cooperation, accumulative learning and sharing with respect for nature. These are concepts that can turn destructive or constructive depending on the value system and the awareness of those who use them. To show the workings the concepts are placed inside the context of events or philosophies.

Three wheels to turn
To deal with the rhizome reality that has no beginning neither an end, the theory of ecolution approaches developments from the middle with a dynamic model that is visualized as a matrix. Three solutionfinding clusters are distinguished: behaviour, technology / institutionalization and decisionmaking. These clusters are connected to concepts (plans for action) to change.

The concepts in the following paragraphs are ordered according to the three solutionfinding clusters that can be perceived as wheels to turn for change.

Developments meander from one phase into another and touch all three clusters, which means that change in one evokes (often unforeseen) changes in the other two as well, and so on, perpetually. So, the three wheels form a kind of machine in which, when one turns the other two turn as well.

For instance the decisionmaking concept democracy can steer a society towards durable governance, but requires conditions such as vigilant citizens, technology to collect and count votes, and institutes that guarantee fair elections.

There are many faces of democracy and its' counterpart dictatorship. The connection between governance and fundamental human needs or deprivations is one of the red threads of the joint effort society, as is the dichotomy (individual) freedoms and order. This already ancient dichotomy needs to be solved over and over. Each society, every era, has to find out for itself, again and again, how to deal with seemingly opposing needs.

For each solutionfinding cluster adequate concepts can be found. The underneath is not a limited summing up. To select new concepts, the paragraph 'Selecting concepts' offers criteria.

In this chapter the turning wheel decisionmaking is discussed. The second solutionfinding cluster focuses on concepts that connect especially to Behaviour, after which Technology & Institutionalization come to the stage.

Who should decide?
*'Legislation won't change the heart, but
it will restrain the heartless.'*
Martin Luther King Jr.

The word democracy is rooted in ancient traditions and has a double meaning. On one hand democracy is a form of governance based on a set of values, rules and principles. On the other side democracy is much more than that: it is a way of life.

The concept democracy goes back 2600 years and was applied first in the area we now know as Iran, Iraq and Syria. '[…] The little word democracy is much older than classical Greek commentators made out. Its roots are in fact traceable to the Linear B script of the Mycenaean period, seven to ten centuries earlier, to the late Bronze Age civilization (c. 1500-1200 BCE) that was centered in Mycenae and other urban settlements of the Peloponnese. It is unclear exactly how and when the Mycenaeans learned to use the two syllable word damos, to refer to a group of powerless people who once held land in common, or three-syllable words like damokoi, meaning an official who acts on behalf of the damos.'[71]

As John Keane described in Life and Death of Democracy the concept changed the world. Keane even stated that it made history possible. 'For understood simply as people governing themselves, democracy implied something that continues to have a radical bite: it supposed that humans could invent and use institutions specially designed to allow them to decide for themselves, as equals, how they would live together on earth.'[72]

Around 510 BCE in Athens the nobility rivaled for the tyranny of the city. Burning ambitions, love affairs and jealousy divided the Aristoi. The fighting and murdering elite rolled over the streets. To complete the chaos, the bloody scramble for power got company from a popular uprising. The man that rose from this turmoil was Cleisthenes, a leader who John Keane called a proto-democrat. For Cleisthenes understood that tyranny founded on fear could never lead to durable government. Among other things, he extended political freedoms downwards, even to those previously denied citizenship. A Council of Five Hundred was installed together with an independent assembly.
'Cleisthenes was the first Athenian ruler of the period to spot that large numbers of people could act in concert, that a demos could exercise initiative, take things into its own hands, without guidance or leadership by aristocrats.'[73]

---

[71] Life and Death of Democracy, John Keane, First published by Simon & Schuster UK Ltd, 2009, Edition Pocket Books 2010, p. xi
[72] Life and Death of Democracy, John Keane, First published by Simon & Schuster UK Ltd, 2009, Edition Pocket Books 2010, p. xi, xii
[73] Life and Death of Democracy, John Keane, First published by Simon & Schuster UK

Roughly 2300 years later President Abraham Lincoln would define democracy not only as government by the people, but also for the people. 'The ideal democratic government would be one whose actions were always in perfect correspondence with the preferences of all its citizens,' Arend Lijphart quoted President Lincoln.[74]

A reasonable responsive democracy guarantees eight institutional freedoms[75]:

1. Freedom to form and join organizations;
2. Freedom of expression;
3. Right to vote;
4. Eligibility for public office;
5. The right to compete for support and votes;
6. Alternative sources of information;
7. Free and fair elections;
8. Institutions for making government policies depending on citizen's preferences (e.g. votes)

The Athenians and their Assembly Democracy had yet another important and guiding concept: 'Democracies require public spaces, open to all, where matters of common concern can be defined and lived by citizens who regard each other as equals.' This civic centre was the agora, where all walked, admired, envied, bought and sold, performed, flirted and felt alive, regardless of differences in wealth and background. The agora was collectively owned and used. It gave the Athenians a sense of 'aidós: meaningful wellbeing and mutual respect'.[76]

This reminds of the goals Amartya Sen set with his Capability Approach: the opportunity to 'live the life one has reason to value'. What we see is that people regardless of time and place (Athens in 500 BCE, the US in 1860's and the UN in 1990's) feel the same passionate desire for: a meaningful life in freedom, dignity with respect for each other and on the base of equality. Democracy is a concept for

Ltd, 2009, Edition Pocket Books 2010, p. 7 - 10

[74] Democracies, Patterns of Majoritarian and Consensus Government in Twenty-One Countries, Arend Lijphart, Yale University Press, 1984, p.1

[75] Democracies, Patterns of Majoritarian and Consensus Government in Twenty-One Countries, Arend Lijphart, Yale University Press, 1984, p. 2

[76] Life and Death of Democracy, John Keane, First published by Simon & Schuster UK Ltd, 2009, Edition Pocket Books 2010, p. 14

decisionmaking that contributes to this desire in various ways.

Power of the state versus freedom of the individual
John Stuart Mill wrote his masterpiece On Liberty in 1859. Mill researched the dichotomy power of the collective versus the power of the individual (order vs. freedom). It came out to be a principal manifest against the primacy of the state, sharply questioning the legitimacy of the power of a society over the freedom of an individual. The battle between individual freedom and collective authority still is relevant. 'The subject of this Essay,' On Liberty begins, 'is not the so-called Liberty of the Will, so unfortunately opposed to the misnamed doctrine of Philosophical Necessity; but Civil, or Social Liberty: the nature and limits of the power which can be legitimately exercised by society over the individual. A question seldom stated, and hardly ever discussed, in general terms, but which profoundly influences the practical controversies of the age by its latent presence, and is likely soon to make itself recognized as the vital question of the future. It is so far from being new, that, in a certain sense, it has divided mankind, almost from the remotest ages, but in the stage of progress into which the more civilized portions of the species have now entered, it presents itself under new conditions, and requires a different and more fundamental treatment.'

The essay produced a number of conditions for the ideal society in the liberal sense and advocated as much individual freedom as possible. According to John Stuart Mill there can be only one reason to limit the freedom of an individual: another individual's freedom. In his opinion a government has but negative power.

Discursive politics
The trias politica was invented to separate political, judicial and executive powers. It is one of the concepts that checks and balances a democratic system to prevent democracy from turning into autocracy and to limit the power of the collective - or one party, one family, one person - over the individual while keeping order. Independent courts have to weigh the individual freedom versus the primacy of the state, among others.
These independent courts got to play the second fiddle more and more often since ending the 1970's conservatism colored the

political and economic landscape. Governments such as the Bush administration in the USA (§ Dictatorship in utero) put security and order first. From the era of Thatcher and Reagan on, the predominance of the legislative, political power gradually had become indisputable. The power of the state over the individual grew in the name of order and security. One example of a law that constrains individual freedom and is in conflict with the right of self-determination[77] is compulsory identification. Police can arbitrarily stop people, ask for it, fine the person who doesn't carry the ID with him or her, or even detain that person. When the ID gets lost, a new one can be obtained at considerable costs - that vary per community - plus a fine. Apart from this, citizens have to fingerprint at city hall. Such a circle-of-regulations is a severe set back of personal freedom. The state requires very intimate information of the individual. The argument is security. Although voices rise to abolish the fingerprint requirements, this still was customary in many Dutch communities in 2011.

This predominance of law and control hasn't always been the case. Until deep in the nineteenth century most administrations had limited powers. The political processes weren't yet institutionalized as today. Those were the days of the discursive politics, a kind of decentralized decisionmaking that left the choice of game rules and procedures to the decisionmakers.[78] The problem with such decentrality is that when issues overarch multiple subjects, many people, or a large area, the decisions easily lead to conflicts. For instance, the department of transport wants to expand the national airport, while the department of environment thinks it is necessary to limit the number of flights. One community plans to build villas in the rural area, while the neighbouring locality wants to turn the same terrain into an area of silence to enhance biodiversity.

Conflicts of interest, chaos, greed, inconsistency and incoherent policies

---

[77] The right of self-determination is established in the international covenant on civil and political rights and in the international covenant on Economic, Social and Cultural Rights, both dating from 1966. The individual right of self-determination is to be perceived as a part of personal freedom and a basic human right.
[78] Political science calls political processes 'discursive' when decisionmakers define among themselves the rules and procedures they follow leading to a decision. Guido Dierickx, De logica van de politiek, uitgeverij Garant, 2005, blz. 89

paralyze decentralized discursive politics. Therefore the answer is sought in overarching, central decisionmaking for society as a whole, instead of compartmental. An integral system becomes the new governing fashion, with the central administration – elected as representatives of the people – as the main decisonmaker and highest power in society. 'Integral' in this case means as much as 'complete integration and control of all discursive processes into one big system'.[79] This system maintains itself in the turbulent environment of discursive processes and even rises stronger then before.[80] The result of such development is an almost untouchable position of power of the state and its' many institutions. 'The current integral systems,' Guido Dierickx wrote, 'have succeeded in accumulating more power tools than the former did. The new communication techniques, larger financial means and modern day organizational methods all contribute to a larger policy power of the government.'[81]

The 'integral system' gave birth to the state under the rule of law of which democracy is lord and master. The game rules to this democracy are[82]:

- The beginning of decisionmaking – selection of issues (agenda setting) is free;
- The conflict is settled as soon as the majority of individual participants support a proposed solution;
- There is no prepositioned, fixed objective that serves as a criterion to judge the value of the policy.

This democracy functions so long as the debates and discourses performed in Parliament and the Administration mirror the societal debates and discourses, after which the representatives update the legislation.
Discourses and democratic decisionmaking have to correspond,'

[79] Guido Dierickx, De logica van de politiek, Uitgeverij Garant, Antwerpen/Apeldoorn, 4th print 2005, p. 102
[80] Guido Dierickx, De logica van de politiek, Uitgeverij Garant, Antwerpen/Apeldoorn, 4th print 2005, p. 102
[81] Guido Dierickx, De logica van de politiek, Uitgeverij Garant, Antwerpen/Apeldoorn, 4th print 2005, p. 122-123
[82] Guido Dierickx, De logica van de politiek, Uitgeverij Garant, Antwerpen/Apeldoorn, 4th print 2005, p. 154-156

A.F.A. Korsten argued in an article on the analyses of discourse. 'The correspondence failed a number of times in the recent past. Whether it concerned education policy or rural development the consensus building of the Dutch model and the stubbornness of administrators combined with a parliament that lacked analyses of its' own produced sub-optimal solutions.'[83]

What happens is that the system maintains itself and eliminates dissent. Moreover, the system enforces itself, just as Donella Meadows warned. The system defends its' own existence. People and organizations with vested interests - inside the system - expand their bases of power, or at least try to sustain these. They have financial means, communication staffs and lobbyists at their disposal to block change. However, to obtain a sustainable - ecological, economic and socio-cultural - development innovation (creative destruction) is necessary. Under the current circumstances there is no sustainable development. And the new and fresh has not yet the institutions - representation of interests, spin doctors, communication experts and needed financial means. It has, on the other hand, the energy and appeal of youth (meaning young in spirit) that is in sharp contrast with the conservative attitude of the economic, ecological, societal and political elites.

History shows how centralistic regimes eventually crumble, explode or implode. The Roman Empire, Hitler's Germany, the USSR all fell. The fiercer the repression, the stronger the resistance. People choose conservatism and compliance when they are afraid of losing what they have, in terms of income, regular jobs or their lives. They accommodate to situations they reasonably cannot avoid. They do so until the tide turns. When bright colors such as orange and yellow enter fashion, Western society is turning optimistic and loses fear.

Democracy has been hovering Earth already for 2600 years. It is one of the concepts that continuously renews and stays. Democracy is, apart from a form of governance, a way of life. The proto-democrat resembles the person who chooses voluntary simplicity based on free will. He or she is not interested in gathering more power over others, but he or she is interested in the Nobody Rules concept. The same

---

[83] Deliberatieve beleidsanalyse en politiek als vorming van discourscoalities, Prof. Dr. A.F.A. Korsten, p.1, March 11 2005

attitude characterizes the voluntary simplicitist who has no interest in gaining as many objects as possible. The voluntary simplicitist has no ambition to own five television sets, three cars or other extravagant gewgaws like the capitalist prodigals that Adam Smith so passionately condemned. The proto-democrat restrains him- or herself. He or she killed the desire for power, just like Mahatma Ghandi advised. 'Who kills the desire, is past the addiction.' Some call democracy the least bad of all governances, but when we decide to vision democracy as a way of life that truly and intrinsic takes into account the interests of minorities and/or weaker members of society, we can but conclude that democracy is a condition sine qua non for ecolution.

That is, until we find a better way to live together. John Keane presumed democracy turned yet another page of development and is in transition, towards governance and mutual decisionmaking that is more relevant to and corresponding with the issues of current times. Democracy is like a well shaped vase: without flowers she is hollow and empty, when filled with a fresh bouquet spring and life enter the room, when the flowers perish and start to rot, it stinks. In short: democracy is what we make of it.

The multiple lives of democracy
Although part of human societies for millennia, democracy suffers backlashes at times and places. It has been threatened, has died according to John Keane[84], and was reborn and kept developing into different forms. Democrats have been looking for checks and balances to prevent one person, family or party, from having absolute power over many (the powerless). In the first half of the twentieth century we have seen how vermin tried to turn democracy into an autocratic dictatorship in Europe.

Adolf Hitler, a classic example, turned discontent and pent-up anger into tools for gaining power and abusing - even exterminating - large groups of the population. Hitler c.s. thrived on the economic malaise Germany fell into due to large repayments imposed on the country after WWI. The Nazi-regime used scape-goating as a technique to unleash the population's discontent. Although this is widely known and

---

[84] Life and Death of Democracy, John Keane, First published by Simon & Schuster UK Ltd, 2009, Edition Pocket Books 2010

broadly condemned even now, more than sixty years after WWII ended, there still are 'adventurers' who abuse the vocabulary of freedom and point in the direction of minorities or 'aliens'[85]. These wannabe tyrants try to obtain a democratic majority through manipulating feelings of discontent or fear, after which they abolish freedoms in the name of security.

A different, more disruptive method to obtain power is through a coup. Both attacks on democracy have been applied over and over. Dictatorship has been dominating the majority of governing bodies for ages. In 1945 the world counted no more than twelve functioning democracies. This amount increased to 32 by 1958. Apart from progress, there was a fall back as well between 1958 and 1975. One third of the countries known as functioning democracies in 1958 had become authoritarian by 1975. Thirteen of the governments in 1962 were the result of a coup and by 1975 the number of military dictatorships had nearly trebled to 38. Among those were countries such as Greece, where Colonel Papadopoulos lead the military junta, Portugal was ruled by dictator Marcello Caetano and Spain suffered from General Franco, while the former Republic of Yugoslavia was brought under the yoke by Marshal Tito.[86] These rulers were ousted by 1975 and one could say this plastered the road for a democratic and united Europe.

However starting the second millennium, the poor and unfortunate that aren't born on European soil had a hard time getting their rights on the continent of the Union. Migration policy is a harrowing example. It differs from one EU country to the other. The country of entrance is the country to apply for a staying permission. Spain, Greece and Italy receive the most refugees due to their geographic position. Reception conditions vary enormously and are bad to evil especially in Greece and Italy. One Ethiopian girl who accidently arrived in Greece amidst the height of arrivals of North African freedom seekers reported how afraid

---

[85] The word 'aliens' is misleading and discriminating when it is being used for people from a different social or cultural background than the majority inside a nation. These people can never be aliens, since they participate in society and are known by their names.
[86] Life and Death of Democracy, John Keane, First published by Simon & Schuster UK Ltd, 2009, Edition Pocket Books 2010, p. 654

she was to walk on the streets.[87] Police was her worst enemy, if she was detected she'd spend months in prison.[88] Her crime: the will to succeed, as John Kenneth Galbraith explained in the Nature of Mass Poverty. All she wanted was meaningful wellbeing and mutual respect, or aidós[89], such as the Athenians found at the agora centuries ago. Now she is stuck and hiding in Athens, dependent on charity and a small job at night, so she can rent a bed and doesn't have to sleep outside. So she can hide during the days, from the Greek police and violent extremists that call themselves Golden Dawn.

Dictatorship in utero

In the Letter of warning to a young patriot The End of America[90] Naomi Wolf warned for the comeback of the company Liar & Hypocrite in national politics, being the Bush administration at that time in 2007.

Wolf characterized ten steps towards autocratic rule that dictators-to-be take when closing an open society. 'The big picture reveals that ten classic pressures - pressures that have been used in various times and places in the past to close down pluralistic societies - were set in motion by the Bush administration to close down our own open society.'[91]

Ten steps from democracy to dictatorship[92]:
1. Invoke an Internal and External Threat;
2. Establish Secret Prisons;

---

[87] From a Skype conversation, October 2012

[88] 'Greece, one of the major gateways into the EU, sharply limits the numbers of people who can apply for asylum every week and leaves vulnerable asylum-seekers on the streets without food or shelter. Migrants, including children, can spend months in detention centres, in conditions that the European Committee for the Prevention of Torture termed, bluntly, "unacceptable." From: EU, as peacemaker, should welcome those fleeing war, by Judith Sunderland and Alice Farmer, Human Right Watch Published in: European Voice, October 17, 2012

[89] An open space for democracy, like the agora in ancient Athens. The agora was collectively owned and used. A space where citizens experienced meaningful wellbeing and mutual respect regardless wealth or status. § Who should decide?

[90] The End of America, Letter of warning to a young patriot, A citizen's call to action, Naomi Wolf, Chelsea Green Publishing Company, Canada, July 2007

[91] The End of America, Letter of warning to a young patriot, A citizen's call to action, Naomi Wolf, Chelsea Green Publishing Company, Canada, July 2007, Introduction

[92] The End of America, Letter of warning to a young patriot, A citizen's call to action, Naomi Wolf, Chelsea Green Publishing Company, Canada, July 2007

3. Develop a Paramilitary Force;
4. Surveil Ordinary Citizens;
5. Infiltrate Citizen's Groups;
6. Arbitrarily Detain and Release Citizens;
7. Target Key Individuals;
8. Restrict the Press;
9. Cast Criticism as Espionage and Dissent as Treason;
10. Subvert the Rule of Law

A sustainable society requires vigilant citizens who develop social and political intelligence. The main enemy of a sustainable society is terror. Dictators and would-be dictators as well as fundamentalists of any sort are specialists in terror. Their power thrives on fear and hatred among groups - 1st step of establishing dictatorship.
The poverty of almost a whole continent, such as Africa, where hunger, illness, depletion of potable water and other misfortunes hit the people, can be explained by many historical and current events, but not in the least by dictatorship. Dictators that stay in power through a paramilitary organization that - without legal reason and without filing charges, or by filing false charges - is licensed to detain people, sometimes for years, in secret prisons. These are the second and third step to establish dictatorship.

Austrian social scientist and writer Eugen Kogon described in his hair-raising book Der SS-Staat how fast and furious events turn society into horror.[93] Mr. Kogon was arrested the first day of Hitler's conquest of Austria, on March 12, 1938. The Gestapo questioned him for one year and a half for he had been interviewing German SS officers in Austria before the country was occupied. Kogon, being a sociologist, researched the structure and command of power. In September 1939 Eugen Kogon was detained in the Lager of Buchenwald. His imprisonment lasted until April 16, 1945, when American forces liberated him and other prisoners.

The American Intelligence knew who he was. They immediately put him to work: Eugen Kogon wrote down his experiences and knowledge of the system of terror. Four hundred pages typed with the most

---

[93] Eugen Kogon, Der SS-Staat, Das System der Deutschen Konzentrationslager, Wilhelm Heyne Verlag, München, 1974

horrendous descriptions of what man is capable of are the result. The descriptions of Eugen Kogon were of such accurateness that the Americans asked him to write more. It took him three weeks to finish half his book. His account affirms the analyses of Naomi Wolf some sixty years later, although there is one enormous difference. Kogon's book breathes the fear the prisoners felt. Der SS-Staat is much more than a report of events, it is a sociological study on terror from deep within. After the book was finished, it shocked the authorities so deeply, that they banned it. Intelligence Agencies of the US and Israel thought it might become a manual for terrorists and dictators. In a way, it is, for Kogon reveals step by step the rise of systematic terror.

In 1974 the book was finally published on insistence of the author. He found it important for the youth to become aware of the literally black pages from European history. Small typography fills each page from top to bottom, leaving hardly a margin and without any pictures except for the map of Buchenwald - on the last page. The form/design is as burdensome as the content, expressing oppression.

We will leave Eugen Kogon here, this is not the place to discuss his impressing account further. The point is, that Kogon like Wolf, warned for repetition of such devolution and urged citizens in society to carefully watch for and correct steps in the direction of dictatorship. Kogon: 'Man muß den Terror in seinen Anfängen, in seinen Erscheinungsformen, in seinen Praktiken und in seinen Folgen entlarven. Denn wir wurden Zeugen davon, und werden es noch immer, wie es sich inmitten heutiger Demokratien entwickelt, wie er zur Macht kommt und sich als Democratie selbst ausgibt, geradezu als eine Regierungsform von Freiheiten.'

Naomi Wolf described how deep the US had sunk since September 2006, when the American Congress voted for the Military Commissions Act. This law gave the President the power to implement a separate and stand-alone juridical system to try hostile, foreign 'fighters'. Under this law torture was defined different and suspects do not obtain the same legal protection as under other, previous, codes. The Military Commissions Act allows arbitrary arrests without filing charges. It also permits lengthy hearings and detention in isolation. Guatánamo became the ghastly symbol.

Criminalize the migrant

The Netherlands has its' own Military Commissions Act in the form of compulsory identification for all from the age of 14, since January 1, 2005. Individuals that cannot proof their identity, can be arrested and detained. This is and has been especially hard on irregular migrated people. The criminalization of the sans papiers had been carefully prepared by all in politics. The Age of Tolerance gradually slipped into the Age of Exclusion. This started somewhere in the late eighties, beginning of the nineties. Politicians of all parties began to use the words 'Illegal' and a little later they started to speak of 'Illegal' and 'Criminal' in the same sentence, as if these were synonyms and a person without proven ID was in fact being illegal and a criminal - not even a suspect, but a proven criminal. In 1998 the Koppelingswet - that can be translated in English as the Linkage Law - was implemented. This law was designed to prevent migrants from taking advantage of the Dutch Welfare State and linked labour to a staying permission, health care to a staying permission, social security to a staying permission, and since the administrations of the diverse institutes got linked, all personal data are available to the diverse governmental institutes. The Linkage Law was designed to exclude people, to protect the Dutch treasury from financial abuse by foreigners, especially from those who come from impoverished countries.

The law on compulsory identification - added up to a series of laws that began with the Linkage Law - confined undocumented migrants to the margin of society. When the police, in a random range of activities - such as traffic control or at a football match - stops an undocumented migrant, there is a special place were he or she is taken: the UC, or deportation centre. Dutch deportation centres can easily be compared to Guantánamo. They form a kind of compiling foreigners' prison for more and quicker deportations. In Rotterdam, in a large barrack, accumulated containers functioned as prison cells until December 2011.[94] The small ones were for one or two persons. Families with children obtained a somewhat larger cell. There was no daylight. The thus detained irregular migrated people were aired one hour a day in bare cages behind blinded gates. There were no sportsfacilities, no other activity programs. Just sitting in the cell for most of the day, until a

---

[94] Website: Vrijheid van Beweging, Fort Nederland in Beeld, Zestienhoven

plane was ready to deport you. This UC closed and was replaced by another one, also in Rotterdam. The new prison has room for 576 men, women and children. It contains 320 cells and 24 isolation cells.[95] The isolation cells contain people who go on hunger strike, who protest or of who are expected to resist deportation. A private security company surveils.

These types of detention centres for innocent people, who committed no other crime than the Will to Succeed and who can contribute to a society if they are only let to do so (participate), are a horrendous kind of ecological illiteracy. It is putting the lives of people on hold, destroying them, denying people, and children, fundamental unalienable human rights, in the name of King / Queen and Country, only because they lack proper papers. The trauma's such imprisonment causes hammer on these lives for years to come. It is the opposite of creating a sustainable society. It is the destructive face of the primacy of the nation state. Such institutional crimes are not confined to the Netherlands, many nations act in similar ways.

In the name of security
In 2010 the events took a strange corner. Hacker activist and founder of the whistleblower site Wikileaks, Julian Assange was declared national enemy of the US and had become an internationally wanted man. The nine years leading up to this event can be characterized by growing security measurements and limitations of individual freedoms throughout the Western part of the world.

After the attack on the Twin Towers by the fundamentalist Al Qaeda group, followed among others by the assault on the early morning packed forensic trains in Madrid on March 11, 2004, the Western fear of Islam was at a peak. Populists and national governments fed the fear. They used External Threat to limit individual freedoms by issuing more and more security laws. Wikileaks exposed secret documents and emails by governments, diplomats and armies, and thus 'threatened national security'. nonfiXe wrote on the website:
'The Angst is fed on a daily basis by politicians crying out loud oneliners on Islam atrocity, thus trying to convince the public of the necessity of

---

[95] Website: Vrijheid van Beweging, Fort Nederland in Beeld, DC Rotterdam

laws restricting every civilians' freedom.

'The restrictions are very well known to all of us, and we have grown used to some of them, so most people don't care anymore: compulsory identification also for kids as young as 14 - body search at airports - fingerprints taken at city hall - camera surveillance in public spaces ... (Surveil ordinary civilians).

'Now Lady Liberty took one more blow, and a severe one: on freedom of press. Western governments are not often seen this united, as they seemed to be on silencing Wikileaks. The organization is being blacksheeped in a classical way, accused of putting lives in danger by opening the big black book of international diplomacy. Congressmen/women, politicians and global leaders, when speaking of Wikileaks use the words "treason" and "criminal". There have been several attempts by governments to shut the site down and to cut of financial resources. (Restrict the press)

'Its' founder Julian Assange, is being hunt down. Yes, for a reason, a good reason if it is true, he is being accused of rape, a severe offense, for which anyone ought to be punished. But, have you ever witnessed a chase on a rapist so very well coordinated, internationally, as this one? Doesn't it at least make one think there are other motives to catch him? Officials have called in public for his assassination. The West put out a "fatwa". (Target key figures)

'The most astonishing part is that so far nobody, except for the former minister of development of the Netherlands - Bert Koenders - has stated that the Wikileaks information is false, untrue. Koenders, rather mildly, spoke of a misinterpretation by the Americans, on his willingness to use development funds for political use.

'Is Wikileaks in her right then? This is another hard to answer question. What do we know about Wikileaks? Who, except Julian Assange, is behind it? Wikileaks prides itself no innocent lives have been endangered by their info torrents. It published the sources together with the news, so readers can make up their own mind. Well-known and prestigious newspapers shared the content. The Guardian, the New York Times, Der Spiegel, El Pais and Le Monde are not the least of the Western papers. They have a long tradition of well-founded journalism. So far Wikileaks seems to have the right on her side.

'But the organization, which has become powerful through the information they obtained and the access they have to a very, very large audience, needs to restrain itself too.

What is the use of revealing locations vital to the US, except if you want to show your muscles? "Look, we know everything about you and we'll spread the info around," they seem to say. Threatening to publish explosive information if anything happens to Julian Assange isn't quite nice either. It is blackmail. Either you publish, because you think people have a right to know, or you don't.

'Conclusion: We need to reread Naomi Wolfs' book and thoroughly watch who we are following, voting for, what laws we accept and which we dismiss in the name of Lady Liberty. To what extend do we let security imprison freedom?

'We have to formulate our own ethics and live by them. Wikileaks succeeded in putting the finger on a weak spot: Democracy today is not as democratic as most think. Power corrupts, therefore those in power need to be accountable for their actions. That is one of the main reasons why freedom of press (and speech) is so damn important.'[96]

Difference of opinion

Individual freedom, of which freedom of expression is a crucial part, appears not to be valued the same throughout the world. And it has not always been as explicit in the Western countries as it is today either. Two generations ago collectivity was considered more a quality than individuality throughout much of Western society as well.

People gather around a religion or tribe that unites and protects them. Individual freedom threatens the herd. The tension between the individual and the community can be felt from both perspectives. Communities tend to muffle dissent and exclude newcomers. Individuals tend to meet the world from an egocentric point of view and cause distress inside a community. The broad perspective on Western society is that it has become a harsh, cold jungle where everybody is just looking out for themselves, not even in contact with their direct neighbours. The warmth of a collective (a family) is dearly missed.

In Muslim countries personal freedom tends to be limited by religious prescriptions that are thought of discriminating and parochial by non-Muslims. Women's rights for example are subject to severe restrictions

---

[96] Freedom of Speech, Caro Sicking for nonfiXe

and criticism. The question however is, are the women in non-Muslim, but poor countries, such as Ethiopia, better off then those in Muslim countries? In numerous situations women pay the price, whether in a Christian, Hindu or Muslim environment.

Even in the developed and rich Western nations women more then often receive a lower salary than men who do the same work. Women in the Netherlands had no right to vote until some hundred years ago. That is just two generations away from the middle-aged population of today, namely the grand mothers of the current parents.

The dichotomy Individuality – Collectivity needs to be solved in a joint effort society. It is one of the divergent problems Schumacher wrote about, that is 'offending the logical mind', but 'without which man would be nothing more than a clever animal'. In a joint effort society these opposing values can be united by the concept Empathy. Empathy attacks egoism and leaves room for individual freedoms. Empathy also allows people to live together, despite apparent differences.

The matrix here would be erected around the concept Empathy, in search for behaviour, technology / institutionalization and decisionmaking that stimulate empathy. For instance in a community that lacks social cohesion people decide together to: talk to the neighbours (behaviour), create some kind of collective space (agora) where people meet (inst. / techn), engage the intended users of the space and let them create such space together (decisionmaking).

The opposite is interesting as well. The economic crisis from 2007/8 continued over the years and affected household incomes and business revenues severely. Governments saved banks that would have collapsed otherwise. Governments saved other governments, whole countries were at the verge of bankruptcy. Consumer's confidence decreased to the point that communities started their own financial subsystem. Financing the Future was the theme of a TEDX meeting in the Dutch city Leiden on November 2, 2012. One of the speakers was the president of the International Reciprocal Trade Association (IRTA) and the Community Connect Trade Association (CCTA), Annette Riggs, from Lafayete, Colorado. The website CCTA states that it is 'an association of professionals and business owners who trade products and services for other things they need. CCTA members reduce expenses and increase sales by doing business with each other without using cash'.

Instead of cash the members use 'trade credits' to buy and sell goods and services from each other. The subsystem had kept companies in business that otherwise would not have survived the economic crises, Mrs. Riggs told her audience in Leiden. Plus, the system enhanced the social cohesion in the community. A good incentive for the matrix sketched above on the neighbourhood that felt it needed more warmth between the people. On the other hand, and this is why we discuss non-cash business and trade here, in a community that has already a supportive and social fabric, the non-cash trade can destruct this. We spoke about the issue with Mrs. Riggs after the meeting. She stated that a social fabric could diminish when people start to calculate. The primer than becomes exchange and the exchange will be measured and has to be repaid each time. Instead of just helping somebody out, which would have been the normal thing to do before, calculations become dominant.

The above shows how each situation and each community has to find out, every time anew, which concepts and what kind of matrix it develops. As is said before, there is not one-solution-fits-all.

Female vocation

We have seen democracy evolving through the ages. There were setbacks and there has been progress. The ultimate democratic concept is 'Nobody Rules'. Which is a concept mankind has never been able to put to action. Many have been, and still are, excluded from political participation and decisionmaking in various ways. The majority of this group of excluded has always been female. In the Netherlands the first generation of women that was allowed to vote, were the grandmothers of the current middle-aged. The female voting right was not established before 1922. The arguments that excluded Dutch grandmothers from political participation must sound familiar to those who are denied political (as well as economic and social) rights today[97]:

- The right to vote is unfeminine. A real woman would never want the right to vote (or be elected)

---

[97] From Aletta Jacobs organisation. Aletta Jacobs was the principal fighter for Dutch female rights.

- Men are sensible and rational by nature, as opposed to women. God created them that way;
- Women are happy as it is, without the right to vote;
- Women who demand the right to vote better obey the law (that excludes them)
- Women's rights are confined to the household where she is master.

Even today, this type of argumentation is used in a modern and free society as the Netherlands. A small fraction in Dutch Parliament holds such abject opinions on women and their rights to enjoy political functions among others. The SGP (Political Reformational Party) that is based on orthodox protestant pillars holds the view that women are not created to govern, get elected or even vote. It took seventy years, after the passage of the right to vote for Dutch women came into practice, before the SGP changed its statutes - under severe societal pressure - and acknowledged the right for women to vote. Adding: 'Should she think it appropriate'. This was in 1989.

Until 2006 women were denied membership of the Reformational party. This party rule was changed after a court sentence. In 2012 the SGP still excluded women from parliamentary seats and governing office, claiming that God created man as the head of women. Female vocation and place lies in other aspects of life (the household and child care) The statutes, regulations and Program of Principles of the SGP were closed documents not downloadable from the parties' website by visitors from outside the party.[98] Excluding people from political participation based on gender, race, religion or status is denying people freedoms, fundamental rights and a violation of fundamental human needs as formulated by the Chilean economist Max-Neef[99].
Moreover the exclusion of political participation is a sign of one group feeling superior to the other. Often the excluded accommodate to this

---

[98] Dutch Section of the International Commission of Jurists: 'In article 10 of the Program of Principles the SGP rejects the passive right to vote for women. Article 7 claims that "God created man first. The woman was taken out of the man. Women are 'subordinate' to the 'responsible' man, but they are not inferior.
[99] Manfred Max-Neef formulated fundamental human needs that overlap societies and ages. The cultural differences are expressed in the way these needs are satisfied. From: Real-Life Economics: Understanding Wealth Creation, ed. Paul Ekins & Manfred Max-Neef, Routledge, London, 1992.The Human Scale Development can also be found on the web.

worldview, like many of the women in SGP dominated communities allegedly do. The issue here is (in)equality, which is often matched with paternalism and/or oppression.

The next paragraph shows how inequality between races (Black & White) can lead to massacres and long-term suffering for the oppressed. This example from the colonial era shows how battlefields of today root in historical traumas. These traumas may not be the sole causes of deprivation and resource depletion, but they explain a lot on how the global society got (dis)organized.

White man's primacy
In the Congo, some one hundred fifty years ago, the Belgium colonist - as much as all other colonizing powers - took a likewise parochial view as the Dutch Reformational Party (SGP). This opinion did not confine to women only, but defined whole local populations as inferior.
The Industrial Revolution had led to increasing needs of raw materials in the West and Africa seemed able to produce these. King Leopold ii wanted a piece of what he called 'the magnificent African pie'. For he reasoned, 'every self respecting kingdom owns a colony'. Discoverer Stanley knew just what kind of territory was still 'free'.

Henri Morton Stanley had been the first European to sail the river Congo and roughly map the thick forest of the surrounding land. Until then colonizers had mainly showed interest in coastal African areas, assuming the centre of Africa was impervious for man. King Leopold, when he heard the good news of Stanley penetrating unknown land, employed him and sent him back to Central Africa. The following five years Stanley was to set up a Belgium infrastructure of trading stations. This was of strategic importance, for states had to demonstrate 'effective control' to claim territory in the colonies.[100]

In 1884 the greedy king gave orders to filch all rights to the land and it's fruits from the local tribal chiefs by contracts written in English or French - an alien language for the Congolese - in return for the famous beads and marbles Europeans used to buy out indigenous people with

---

[100] Katie Willis, Theories and Practices of Development, Second edition, Routledge Perspectives on Development, 2011 p. 24 **Willis, K. (2011).**

all over. Once the stations were established evangelists quickly followed to 'save the souls of the poor spiritual straying black population'.

But this was not before Stanley had returned to his Belgium king loaded with papers that signed off the land to Leopold. Together, sitting in the royal villa at the North Sea coast, the king and the discoverer drew lines with a red pencil on the map of Africa. While looking over the beach and presumably drinking a good glass of wine, they arbitrarily created a nation to satisfy Leopold's hunger for land. This small gathering on August 7 1884, of two men in Oostende, Belgium, changed the course of millions of lives thousands of miles away. It would lead to the death of ten million Congolese[101]. France, Great Britain and the other European powers accepted Leopold's claim in 1885, at the Berlin Conference where Europe divided the world among itself.

The trading posts that were owned by Leopold all waved the same flag: blue with a shiny yellow star. The blue symbolized the darkness in which the Congolese population roamed. The yellow star was the bright light of civilization that Leopold brought to them.[102]
This little story, exemplary for many during the colonist era, marks the superiority that Westerners felt over others. Some colonists behaved like good fathers, others acted abusively, but all of them were convinced of the inferiority of the populations they so conveniently ruled and exploited. The white man's primacy was amongst the most destructive paradigms in that era.

Apart from white supremacy, Africans suffered from Arabian slave drivers that rode up into the inner lands, sailed the rivers in swift boats and caught men, women and children to serve in Muslim households. The slave traders in Congo were thorns in the side of Leopold and Stanley, who were in a hurry to occupy as much land as fast as they could. The excuse to fight against the Arab slavers was a convenient lie that silenced opponents.

In 1908 the king was forced to turn his private toy Congo over to the

---

[101] Adam Hochschild, King Leopold's ghost, a story of greed, terror and heroism in colonial Africa, first published in 1999 by Macmillan, paperback edition, Pan Books, 2012 Hochschild, A. (2012).
[102] David van Reybrouck, Congo, De Bezige Bij, 2010 p. 64

Belgium state. Before he gave up his piece of 'African pie', Leopold ordered to burn all documents. The bonfire in Brussels alone lasted for more than a week. 'I will give them my Congo,' Leopold said, 'but they have no right to know what I did there.'[103] Adam Hochschild called this the politics of forgetting to create silences in history. Although official history has been erased for the largest part, the saying 'to send someone to harvest rubber' is still common today in the Mongo tongue (Congo). It means: 'to tyrannize'.

The colonial era decided the shape and form of many a country and region, of multiple communities and their interrelationships throughout the world of today. The Leopold-example is just one of many that can be used to illustrate the scramble for Africa - and for many other parts of the non-Western world. Colonization changed the social structures, political and economic systems, and cultural values in many places both North and South. The legacy of these changes continued into independence.[104]

The dark side of aid

Africa turned into a lost continent, despite (or perhaps because of) the available resources and the enormous sums of money that are transferred as development aid, according to Dambisa Moyo[105]. Moyo counted a number of causes. Governmental aid has been a powerful tool for Western countries to enforce their political interests in African countries, i.e. buy the ally. Besides this, aid costs money. Interest and pay back dollars haunt the African states. Free market and privatization (i.e. competition) gave African economies the freedom to succeed, but to fail as well, from the mid eighties on, Moyo stated. Apart from this, cruel dictators and greedy regimes profited from the aid money. It

---

[103] Adam Hochschild, King Leopold's ghost, a story of greed, terror and heroism in colonial Africa, first published in 1999 by Macmillan, paperback edition, Pan Books, 2012, p. 294

[104] Katie Willis - Theories and Practices of Development - claims there are three reasons to take colonialism into account when discussing development: 1) It left the world today with many linkages and special bonds between former colonizers and colonized 2) Neo-colonialism: This term is used to describe global relationships which reflect the dominance of the North over the South, despite legal independence. 3) Colonisation changed the social structures, political and economic systems, and cultural norms in both North and South. The legacy of these changes continued into independence. However the third argument covers both previous points.

[105] Dead Aid, Dambisa Moyo, Allen Lane, an imprint of Penguin Books, 2009

provided them with absurd luxury amidst a starving and oppressed people. Hosni Mubarak from Egypt and Ben Ali from Tunisia, for example, were accused of rampant corruption and filling their pockets with money and assets from investors as well as aid money for years. They were good friends of Western governments, keeping the Muslim community down in return for many a favour. From the 1990's on the governance question has become determinant; rampant corruption and weak institutionalization were seen as the reason for economic misery. In other words, institutionalization, decisionmaking, and behaviour, all three solutionfinding clusters of the ecolution matrix, were, and are, in many cases in the destruction phase.

Democracy became the key-solution and pop singers, actors and celebrities entered the aid market, according to Dambisa Moyo. 'Scarcely does one see Africa's (elected) officials or those African policymakers charged with the development portfolio offer an opinion on what should be done, or what might actually work to save the continent from its regression. This very important responsibility has, for all its intents and purposes, and to the bewilderment and chagrin of many an African, been left to musicians who reside outside Africa.'[106]

Moyo claimed that Africa's failure to generate sustainable growth, by which she meant economic growth - has to do with geographical, historical, cultural, tribal and institutional interconnected factors. Democracy and a multi party system, however is not the solution for Africa, Moyo argued. She stated that a benevolent dictator is more equipped to do the job. Just as the Romans thought, and they in fact installed dictators, as if it were interim managers, to guide the Roman Empire through rough times. The variety of the population in African countries requires such (benevolent) dictatorial governance according to Moyo. She overlooked the variety in democratic governance methods. On the two most common for nation states, a majoritarian democracy and the consensus democracy Arend Lijphart wrote in Democracies. 'A majoritarian democracy (two party or Westminster model) is especially appropriate for, and works best in, homogeneous societies, consensus democracy is more suitable for plural societies.'[107] Dambisa Moyo admitted that dictators are easy to find, but the benevolence of these tyrants is a more rare quality. She believes in the primacy of the

---

[106] Dead Aid, Dambisa Moyo, Allen Lane, an imprint of Penguin Books, 2009, p. 27
[107] Democracies, Arend Lijphart, Yale University Press, 1984 p 3/4

economy: 'Democracy is not the only route to economic triumph. [...]
On the contrary, it is economic growth that is a prerequisite for
democracy; and the one thing economic growth does not need is aid.'[108]
The solutions Moyo came up with were Micro lending - banking the
unbankable -, stimulating remittances and unlocking vast resources
(land, saved gold). Apart from the fact that these are not new solutions,
Moyo is wrong on two aspects:

1. Good - transparent, inclusive and controllable - governance is
   needed to make the outcomes of a development available to the
   poor. Those who are bullied around the most are the first to fall
   victim to corruption, because power corrupts. Uncontrolled power
   is dangerous. Checks and balances have to prevent power abuse and
   attack corruption. Dictatorship is famous for its' lack of checks,
   balances and transparency, even benevolent dictatorship;
2. Economic growth is not per sé a generator of development.
   Great peril hides in the neglect of social, ecological and political
   processes[109].

Developing countries where the majority of the world's poor reside
get growth impulses from those who did not accommodate and broke
away. The diaspora often is providing for those who stayed in the
country of origin. Migrants are bottom-up change-agents. They
support their families, can bring new ideas, paradigms and
technologies and sometimes are able to invest in larger projects such
as schools. Remittances flow straight to the intended people: the
mother who needs health care, the sister who needs education.

Galbraith already in the 1960's stated that migration benefits the
country of origin as well as the country of destination.[110] The migrant
is the one who deconstructs. She or he decides not to accommodate
and is many times even prepared to risk his or her life for a better
future. In the following paragraphs we take an in depth look on
remittances in combination with development to find out if these lead
to construction.

---

108 Dead Aid, Dambisa Moyo, Allen Lane, an imprint of Penguin Books, 2009, p. 42/43
109 Manfred Max-Neef, Human Scale Development, Conception, Application and
Further Reflections, 1993. See the website.
110 J.K. Galbraith, The nature of Mass Poverty, Pelican Books, 1987

Return to sender

The worldwide remittances sent through official channels were $440 billion, in 2010. Of this $440 billion $325 billion remittance is estimated to go to developing countries.[111]

In the overview of the World Bank report Remittance and Markets in Africa, the editors stated: 'Remittances are often said to be the most tangible and least controversial link between migration and development (Russell 1992; Ratha 2007). Remittance flows to developing countries have increased substantially during the past decade to reach $325 billion in 2010 (World Bank 2011). Remittances sent by 31 million international African migrants reached nearly $40 billion in 2010, equivalent to 2.6 percent of Africa's gross domestic product (GDP).

'The data on African migration and remittance flows, however, are likely to be understated because of the scale of undocumented migration within the African continent, the large amount of informal remittance channels within the region, and the relatively weak official data in many African countries (World Bank 2006). The true size of remittance flows to Africa, including unrecorded flows through formal and informal channels, is believed to be significantly larger than the official data. After foreign direct investment (FDI), recorded remittances are the African continent's largest source of foreign inflows.'[112]

This money flow is directly allocated where it is needed. It funds the education of brothers and sisters, provides for health care of sick family members, the buying of land or building a house et cetera.[113] This is in

---

[111] World Bank's Migration and Remittances Factbook 2011

[112] Remittance Markets in Africa, World Bank, editing: Sanket Mohapatra & Dilip Ratha, 2012 p. 27

[113] 'A cross-country analysis of 56 developing countries found that higher remittances per capita were associated with greater access to private treatment for fever and diarrhea and that remittances complemented foreign health aid in poor countries (Drabo and Ebeke 2010). A cross-country analysis of 84 countries (46 countries with quintile-level data) found that remittances reduced overall child mortality but tended to be more effective in reducing mortality among children from the richest households than from the poorest households.' [...]Migration enables households to diversify their sources of income and thus reduce their vulnerability to risks such as drought, famine, and other natural disasters.18Migration and remittances have been a part of coping mechanisms adopted by African households facing shocks to incomes and livelihoods (Block and Webb 2001). [...]Remittances can also enable recipient households to build stronger and more resilient housing. [...] Remittances can play an important role in improving access to information and communication technology. Remittance Markets

sharp contrast to the allocation of most official development funds through foreign aid and NGO's. For these funds flow through governments and frequently are used to benefit international policy. This means that befriended dictators of donating countries get their hands on the money first and have the power to decide where it goes - into their own pockets and into the wallets of those who support them. The world has seen the extreme wealth of ousted President of Egypt Mubarak and his family. Thirty percent of the countries' economy was in their hands. In Ethiopia the circus group Afrisinia (then called circus Addis Ababa) was a local NGO to provide street children with extracurricular education and skills. Unicef, Oxfam Novib and Western governments donated large sums of money[114] that according to the testimonies of the group asking for asylum in the Netherlands, mostly disappeared into the pockets of the ministers of State, police officers and members of the board.

France, the fifth migrant-receiving country in the world in 2008, worked with the concept co-development, focusing on empowerment of the migrant and promoting diaspora entrepreneurship and transfer.
One of France's motivations to start the co-development program was to reduce migration. This has been on the sometimes more and at other times less hidden agenda of the French government, throughout the years. It worked only partial, depending on the migrant sending country.

Codevelopment is the process through which immigrants contribute to the socioeconomic development of their country of origin while assimilating into the country to which they have immigrated, to the mutual benefit of both countries.[115] According to Marion Panizzon it 'introduces a type of mutual collaboration that goes beyond the state-centric, classic North-South transfers of development aid disbursed within the strict confines of intergovernmental cooperation. Codevelopment overcomes the bipolar model of migration, which

---

in Africa, World Bank, editors: Sanket Mohapatra and Dilip Ratha, 2012, p. 22/23
[114] Original source, Oxfam Novib website. The document has been removed, but is made available here.
[115] Diaspora for Development in Africa, World Bank, 2012, France's Codevelopment Program: Financial and Fiscal Incentives to Promote Diaspora Entrepreneurship and Transfers, Marion Panizzon p. 183

separates sending from receiving areas, and push factors of out-migration from pull factors of in-migration. Instead, codevelopment operationalizes the theory of migrant transnationalism, which conceptualizes the migrant as a "go-between" between identities, cultures, societies, spaces, and markets. Pursuant to this model, the migrant is conceived as an "agent of change" and the process of migration is viewed as "deterritorialized" from nation states. Thus codevelopment policy relies on and promotes circular migration, but clashes with the more "classic" assimilation / integration policies of migration.'[116]

The behaviour of migrants (sending money home) is stimulating the household income of their families. The French have been creating institutions and regulations to support this development. Apart from this, remittances do not disappear into the deep pockets of dictatorial regimes, or are being used to 'buy the ally'.

The concept Circular Migration is an interesting view on migration as well. It means as much as regularly travelling between the countries of origin and destination, initiating a flow of ideas, goods, services and / or money.

Solidarity development
Codevelopment went through different stages. In 2008 the program got a partner called Solidarity Development. This was meant to add value to the Codevelopment program that departed from the principle of 'joint responsibility'. The Solidarity program - a government-to-government funding program - among others targeted on widening the financial toolkit and focused on regular labour migration.
Marion Pannizon: 'Solidarity development financially supports educational, vocational, and professional training for specific sectors in the source country, such as agriculture, fishery, and health (Tasca 2008:19). It is government-to-government funding of development initiatives with an emphasis on reducing migratory root causes, like unemployment. Unlike codevelopment funding, which is directly disbursed to private parties, that is, to diaspora members, solidarity

---

[116] Diaspora for Development in Africa, World Bank, 2012, France's Codevelopment Program: Financial and Fiscal Incentives to Promote Diaspora Entrepreneurship and Transfers, Marion Panizzon p. 184

development qualifies as structural aid, meaning the type of development aid that is directly granted to a government in a long-term effort, as opposed to short-term disaster relief or humanitarian aid.[117]

During that year, 2008, the French authorized €30 million to co-development projects. In the same period migrants in France remitted €8 billion to African countries of origin. There have been fiscal adjustments to smoothen remittances, such as tax breaks for migrants that set up an investment in their source country, a bank passbook, co-financing of collective investments, access to microcredit facilities and support from the multi-donor solidarity development facility[118] and the co-development prize (institutionalization).

Pannizon for the World Bank: 'The new fiscal instruments are promising, because migrants are encouraged to bancarize their savings, which in turn helps to develop the banking sector in migrants' countries or origin. More critical is the fact that the French Government identifies, often without consulting the country of origin, the type of products into which migrants must invest in order to obtain the tax break. The new strategy of individualizing co-development aid by offering tax breaks to migrants' savings has shifted the paradigm by relying less on migrant communities and more on an individual migrant's responsibility.' Further on in the conclusions of the same essay: 'The new policy mix, known under the labels of co-development, solidarity development, and decentralized government cooperation, and framed by France's immigration laws and its new pacts, has the potential to create the right incentives for migrants to contribute to their source countries' development and to mobilize their governments to match their investments'.[119]

France is said to have found an innovative approach to development and migration. The strategy changed over the years from

[117] Diaspora for Development in Africa, World Bank, 2012, France's Codevelopment Program: Financial and Fiscal Incentives to Promote Diaspora Entrepreneurship and Transfers, Marion Panizzon, p. 194/195

[118] Partnership of the African Development Bank, International Fund for Agricultural Development and the French organization MIIINDS

[119] Diaspora for Development in Africa, World Bank, 2012, France's Codevelopment Program: Financial and Fiscal Incentives to Promote Diaspora Entrepreneurship and Transfers, Marion Panizzon, p. 219/220

development aid to co-development with diaspora, into a mix of government-to-government funding combined with individual incentives, while enhancing banking institutes in receiving countries. It is commonly known that remittances to Africa are the most expensive. They cost up to 15% of the amount of money remitted. By combining migrant empowerment with governmental incentives France has been trying to reduce development aid budgets, reduce tension with former colonies as well as irregular migration. This approach - with all its' pros and cons - might result in a mutual winning situation for France itself, migration source countries as well as individual citizens and companies in both territories.

Empowerment of individuals reduces vulnerability and fights poverty and the evil side effects that come with it, such as slavery and trafficking. Empowerment of the individual however, is most likely to be seized by those who choose to take opportunities and use them to break free. 'Empowerment is something that comes from within', Katie Willis stated in Theories and Practices of Development.[120]

---

[120] Katie Willis, Theories and Practices of Development, Second edition, Routledge Perspectives on Development, 2011 p. 113

Behaviour

Introduction
Behaviour is the second solutionfinding cluster in the theory of ecolution. In the following paragraphs you will find concepts, examples of behaviour and how to turn this wheel for change. The type of behaviour discussed concerns both individual as well as communal or organizational behaviour. Both influence each other. Like Erich Fromm stated: 'a society tells people what they want'. At the same time the individuals create their own society. This circle of influence gets even more complicated when decisionmaking and technology / institutionalization and large marketing budgets or influential lobbyists are taken into consideration as well. The systems can limit individual freedoms, however each individual can choose to rise above the systems he or she is in. To be able to make such a choice, people have to be(come) (self)aware.

I came to be free
The argument that cultures have different values is frequently used to deny an individual's entitlement to unalienable rights. Freedom of expression, speech and thought, freedom of religion, and likewise individual freedoms, are desired by each man and woman indifferent of cultural backgrounds. The people involved should be able to participate in the discourse on restrictions of such freedoms. At what point does freedom of expression become a gross insult and painful to others? Or: where does one individual's right conflict with the rights of others? The choice between values and the prioritizing of freedoms are personal choices, not decisions that should be made for somebody by somebody else.

The freedom to make personal choices is a concept that fits into the Nobody Rules principle of the proto-democrat that is spoken of in the chapter on governance (§ Discursive politics). Decisionmaking and behaviour touch each other very clearly at this point. Democracy is also a way of life. A true democracy needs vigilant civilians - who are aware of the needs of others in society as well - just as much as proto-democrats that represent these citizens. A democracy can only be sustained when all involved respect each other and feel empathic towards each other. Otherwise the majority will dictate society.

Democracy and free, aware and active individuals are inseparable. This brings educational issues, equality in participation and income distribution, ecological literacy, no arms (peace) but consultation to the table. However complex it may seem, when individual freedom is the concept, there are many supporting action plans to think off. The solutionfinding cluster technology / institutionalization will come up with checks and balances to guarantee each individual has access to her or his unalienable freedoms. The rise of the social media enables direct democracy. President Obama of the US understood this opportunity very well, as you can read in § Direct Democracy.

There is some evidence that people prefer freedom before material needs. Amartya Sen wrote about American slaves that were better off from an economic point of view than most single small farmers at the time. Still, after slavery was abolished the majority of the freed men and women denied the offer of their former owners to come back to work in the gang system on the basis of payments that more than doubled the wage from before.[121]

Our own experience teaches the same. Sixteen youth - musicians and acrobats - of Circus Afrisinia came from Ethiopia to the Netherlands for a tour. As soon as the possibility rose, all ran from their guardians and asked for asylum. The reason they gave: Freedom. This happened in May 2007.
The group existed of six girls and ten boys. Their ages varied between 13 and 24 years. Together they formed a musical band and acrobatic dancing group. Their brilliant youth and shining ambition to perform the best they could, made them an attractive beautiful bunch. After their defection they spent a few days in prison at Schiphol Airport, before they were relocated. The minors came to live in the north of the Netherlands. The eleven that were over eighteen were housed in an asylum centre in the south. Now they were officially 'in procedure'. Each of them got their own lawyer to defend their individual application for asylum. This is one of the reasons why things got ugly. The lawyers, who were spread all over the country, did not communicate with each other, although the general stories of abuse all children talked about, confirmed individual claims. Cooperating lawyers

---

[121] Amartya Sen, Development as Freedom, Oxford University Press, 1999, p. 29

would have gained asylum for all and thus led to construction. In this case the one-man shows of the lawyers, who kept each other in the dark, was a form of destructive behaviour.

For the Ethiopian group the whole juridical process was abracadabra, but they trusted that Western values would be applied to them and that it would be a matter of months before they could take off in a new life of freedom. Their optimism made them strong, they practiced and trained and started to perform again. They became a wanted act at many festivals and in theatres. The success lasted until the summer of 2009. Then the first rejection dropped in. Then the second asylum request was denied, and so on. A governmental service, founded to pressure migrants to return to their home countries, got wind of the prospect to kill sixteen birds with one stone. The Repatriation and Departure Service[122] turned the heat on and demanded also minors to their office next to a high walled pre-deportation centre. Fear of deportation paralyzed the young circus group. They stopped performing, lost interest in training and gradually became grey and empty-eyed like most asylum seekers in the country. There is no doubt whatsoever that the Dutch Government is guilty of killing the spirit of these young talented people. The institutions, such as Immigration & Naturalization Service (IND), Central Agency for the Reception of Asylum Seekers (COA), Migration Police (VD) and the Repatriation and Departure Service (DT&V) applied legislation to the end of destruction.

Afrisinia, through their lawyer - all individual cases were finally brought into the hands of one advocate - sent an application to the European Court of Human Rights. This application laid patiently gathering dust at some desk in Strassbourg until five or six years have passed. In the meantime the young become older and their chances to lead a fulfilling and productive life diminish. They are not able to develop their capabilities, such as Amartya Sen described and on which we will come back later.

After five years in the Netherlands and rejected refuge, the young Ethiopians of Circus Afrisinia felt cornered and limited in their development. Those who had families in Addis Ababa dearly missed

---

[122] Dienst Terugkeer en Vertrek

them. When a mother fell sick, a father died, a sister delivered a baby or a brother got married, the longing for home got even more painful. Although working was not allowed for sans papiers, the young artists found irregular jobs to stay alive. Some of them earned quite a sum of money that allowed them to rent a room, even buy smart phones and other gadgets. They enjoyed the materialistic perquisites of the Dutch society and participated in the informal economy. Basic needs, even health care, sports and learning the Dutch language, were covered with the help of volunteers and refugee aid organizations. But waiting in the coulisses of society until the ECHR decided on their future was unsatisfying.

The call for freedom cannot be silenced, not even at the risk of great perils. Human genius is resourceful in looking for escapes and growing hope and this is what happened.

'I came here to be free,' she stated sitting straight and looking determined. 'I got more clothes than I ever could dream of when I lived in Ethiopia. I have telephones and a magnetron. The work I do keeps me alive and provides me with friends. My bosses are nice to me.' She paused to sigh. 'But I feel as if I am living in an open air prison. My life is depressing. I am less free than I was in Ethiopia. This is not why I came. I miss my mother. I have decided to go back.'[123]

The 24 year-old took a brave decision. For she knew there was a reasonable risk she would end up in an Ethiopian prison. Still she went. But she took her precautions. She entered her home country under an alias, with false papers. She immediately reported to the Dutch Embassy in Addis Ababa and requested a so-called Stay with Partner. After succeeding for the test foreigners have to take[124], she was granted permission to reside in the Netherlands, with partner. Now she could travel between here and there, start to study and participate in society and in the formal economy.

All is well that ends well?
There are a few things to consider in this story. First of all, an abused youth - for she like the others was repeatedly raped and had been forced

---

123 From a conversation with one of the performers of Afrisinia
124 Inburgeringsexamen / Integration exam

to work in bondage from early childhood on - has been denied every basic right thinkable when she came asking for help.

Second, the impact of such denial to her call for help - on top of previous traumatic experiences - on the life of a youngster is immense and can be decisive for her future life.

Third, her escape, the only one she could think of, put her in yet another dependent situation, namely that of an unequal relationship with a Dutch man. Should he, within five years, decide he is fed up with her and end the relationship, she will be deported to Ethiopia. This is the same type of power in a relationship that traffickers use. The power is on one side and one side only. The girl put her destiny in a man's hands and he can do how he pleases. That is the price for freedom she has been willing to pay.

The above story is one example of a multitude of similar ones. The reason for telling it here is to stress the importance of freedom despite cultural, social, economical and political differences. Individual people take enormous risks to be free.

The will to succeed

Expectations influence human behaviour and decisionmaking. People who live in a hopeless situation give in to it, because they feel helpless, powerless over their own lives and unable to change their circumstances. They choose to accommodate, a completely rational choice. We owe the term accommodation to John Kenneth Galbraith.[125] Galbraith's The Nature of Mass Poverty characterized the generation long (sometimes centuries long, as is the case in the Bihar region in India) depletion people find themselves in. The equilibrium of poverty hampers people to get out of the cruel circumstances/systems they are in. Galbraith, who was searching for means to eliminate poverty, described the context/system extremely poor people are in as forces that make poverty self-perpetuating. These forces consist among others in the fact that doubling a negligible income results in a still negligible income, while the consumption rises. 'Such improvement as there may be is soon absorbed by the forces - higher survival rate, more births - that re-establish the previous equilibrium. Accommodation to the

---

[125] John Kenneth Galbraith, The Nature of Mass Poverty, first printed in 1979 by Harvard University Press, Published in Pelican Books 1980. Reprinted in 1984 and 1987

culture of poverty is also unchanged. This, in turn, reinforces the equilibrium of poverty by repressing aspiration.'[126]
Aspiration, the construction phase, is explained as 'the will to succeed'. John Kenneth Galbraith argued that when success is continuous out of reach, people by nature stop reaching for it. The absence of the will to succeed (or accommodation)[...] 'is a profound predictable element of human behaviour because it is the refusal to struggle against the impossible, the tendency to prefer acquiescence to frustration.'[127]

The same psychological mechanism lies underneath motivation approaches and the triple loop-learning concept. The other side of the destructiveness of repeated failure is the constructiveness of repeated success.

To escape the poverty equilibrium accommodation needs to be attacked. A smell of success, a hinge of progress, the breakout of a peer, are among the weapons, mostly taken up by a few.
The people who refuse to succumb to accommodation are the avant-gardes, that is, minorities trying to run from the poverty trap, which is binding the society they find themselves in. Most escape through migration. And, 'the more they succeed, the more the logic and rationality of the accommodation declines'.[128]

Accommodation is not confined to impoverished regions. Everybody who once visited an asylum seeker centre (AZC) in the Netherlands has seen it in the eyes of the people living there. The brave migrants who left their homes and tried to break the equilibrium of poverty are slowly throttled in the lengthy procedure that must provide them a permission to stay, work and receive education, if appropriate. During these waiting years, they are allowed just that: to wait. Although there are multiple facilities and, for example, sportsutilities present, most of the time these

[126] John Kenneth Galbraith, The Nature of Mass Poverty, first printed in 1979 by Harvard University Press, Published in Pelican Books 1980. Reprinted in 1984 and 1987, p. 63
[127] John Kenneth Galbraith, The Nature of Mass Poverty, first printed in 1979 by Harvard University Press, Published in Pelican Books 1980. Reprinted in 1984 and 1987, p. 56
[128] John Kenneth Galbraith, The Nature of Mass Poverty, first printed in 1979 by Harvard University Press, Published in Pelican Books 1980. Reprinted in 1984 and 1987, p. 58/59

stay behind locked doors. Not even the employees of the centre know of such existence.[129]

Refugees in the Netherlands are imprisoned, moved from one place to the other on a day's notice, they have to stamp at least once a week, sometimes even more frequently than that, and the more. All of these are measures that deeply interfere into private lives and profoundly injure someone's self-esteem. The system is designed to break people's will before they can enter society. If they can ever enter society. The rejected either leave voluntarily, are put in custody pending deportation, or become 'illegal'.

Here too there are people who decide to break the chains that keep them from living the life they value. Miki was such a chainbreaker. After living in the shadows for five years, he planned to try his luck elsewhere. Europe is a no go for an asylum seeker who has already been denied a staying permission in one of the EU countries. So Miki thought about leaving for the US. Through facebook he reconnected with a former girlfriend from his home country. She had been living in the States for ten years already and earned a decent living. They spoke of getting married. A few months later, Miki went to the diverse embassies, the International Organisation for Migration (IOM) and the Immigration Service. He applied for stay with partner in the US and was admitted. One early morning in October, on a rainy, dark day typical of autumn two cars with friends, Miki and his two suitcases rode to the airport. Everybody was quiet, as if underway to attend a funeral. The traffic was busy, forcing the cars to stop and go. A few kilometres before Schiphol came in sight, a car ran into Miki's, sending a shock through all passengers. The sturdy blow was a perfect fit to the situation. It was the physical expression of their uneasy feelings. At the airport the IOM officer immediately took Miki to the migration police for questioning. The group silently walked along. Some stayed behind, trying to hide their emotions. This departure to freedom was a mixed one. Miki, leaving loved ones for the second time in his young life of 25 years, was stepping into yet another unknown future and was well aware of the

---

[129] This information came from a COA employee who wants to remain anonymous. He said: 'When we were closing the centre, we had to move everything and clean up. I was surprised to find perfectly new sportsmaterials, neither I nor my colleagues knew it was there. I didn't cry, although I wanted to. We threw it all away. COA neither sells anything nor gives it away.'

fact that he would probably never see his brothers and sisters, here gathered, again. These brothers and sisters were in the same situation he was stepping out, they lived the lives of the undocumented. The group stopped in front of the police office. Time to say Goodbye. The force of the gathered was easy to sense. It said: 'Don't go, don't leave'. It also said: 'Good luck brother. We love you'. The IOM officer discretely looked away trying to avoid feeling the agony that hung over the small group. Then the door opened. An apparently indifferent bald policeman in uniform looked at Miki and his farewell party. Miki entered. For questioning. Answering the obvious Immigration already knew for a long time. Questions such as: When did you arrive in the Netherlands? How long have you been here? But also: Where did you live? The answer to the last question could betray his comrades with whom he shared a room. Miki was held for one hour and a half. He nearly missed his plane. After it finally took off, with him on board, the others breathed deep. The first step into a new life was set.

Miki's breakaway from an undesired much troubled situation takes guts and doesn't guarantee glory. But it accounts for two things:
The (Dutch) asylum procedure is a counterproductive legislation, pushing people into the rational thing to do, which is: give up on a lost battle. But the destructive system does not succeed always, many irregular migrated do not give up and a shadow society grows. Plus, the other fact: the Netherlands suffered a loss by letting such a determined young man like Miki leave. Whereas the US wins a citizen with proven will to succeed.

Migration is a type of deconstruction - leaving everybody and everything behind and starting anew in a foreign country. Revolution, of course, is deconstruction as well. According to John Kenneth Galbraith deconstruction is performed by those who have aspiration -the will to succeed. Those people are the ones that attack accommodation. When they succeed, others will follow their example. Galbraith explained multiple times that migration benefits destination countries as well as countries of origin, and the individual migrant. He wrote down one of the most prevalent conclusions that many ignore: the migrant is the strong person, the one seeking change and prepared to leave everything she knows and loves behind to start a new life. Galbraith: 'It is undisputed that they [migrants] brought prosperity to their destination land. The selection was a natural one: those who rejected the accommodation left.'[130] And: 'Migration is the oldest action against poverty. It selects those who most want help. It is good for the country to which they go; it helps to break the equilibrium of poverty in the country from which they come. What is the perversity in the human soul that causes people so to resist so obvious a good?'[131]

Apparently the Dutch government never read The Nature of Mass Poverty by John Kenneth Galbraith, nor any works by Amartya Sen for that matter. The authorities expelled the young Ethiopians of Circus Afrisinia and with them many, many others that would have contributed to society. Apparently not only the Dutch government, but many others too hold the same perversity that causes 'so to resist so obvious a good'.

Closing borders and contra-revolutions that kill the spirit of the first uprising do not lead to construction. Then destruction follows deconstruction, at the risk of rooting accommodation even deeper. The reasons of the perverse exclusion of migrants are to be found in fear for social disturbance and conflict, which happens 'although acculturation usually quickly occurs and tensions subside'[132]. The reasons can be sought in economics: 'they' come to take 'our' jobs. This however is a classical economic error, as Galbraith explained, for the available employment is no fixed quantity and 'the economy does, of course, grow with the labor force and with increasing returns'.[133]

---

[130] John Kenneth Galbraith, The Nature of Mass Poverty, first printed in 1979 by Harvard University Press, Published in Pelican Books 1980. Reprinted in 1984 and 1987, p. 101

[131] John Kenneth Galbraith, The Nature of Mass Poverty, first printed in 1979 by Harvard University Press, Published in Pelican Books 1980. Reprinted in 1984 and 1987, p. 109

[132] John Kenneth Galbraith, The Nature of Mass Poverty, first printed in 1979 by Harvard University Press, Published in Pelican Books 1980. Reprinted in 1984 and 1987, p. 110

[133] John Kenneth Galbraith, The Nature of Mass Poverty, first printed in 1979 by Harvard University Press, Published in Pelican Books 1980. Reprinted in 1984 and 1987, p. 110

Timing revolution

In the World Report of 2012 Human Rights Watch pays a lot of attention to the biggest change in recent history, the people's revolution in the Middle East, known as the Arab Spring. This region wide revolt against thug governments and kleptomaniac abusive autocrats that have been supported by Western elected governments for what seemed an endless time is the ultimate deconstruction and paradigm shift of past years. The uprising of the Arab people changed the global balance of power that has not returned to equilibrium two years later.

'This is a uprising for dignity,' a Tunisian man tells filmer Mongi Farhani, when taking shots for his documentary 'Al Sharara', the Fuse. Farhani, a Dutch Tunisian, tried to recapture what happened in his region of birth that set the whole area ablaze. Fruit vendor Mohammed Bouazizi's self-immolation after another daily, even routinely, offense by the local authorities was the last straw. Apparently nobody saw it coming, not even human rights activists. Eric Goldstein wrote in his essay for HRW: 'We failed to predict the Arab Spring because we were more focused on supply than demand when it came to human rights; that is, we were more attuned to the extent to which governments supplied (or did not supply) the chance to exercise basic rights than we were with the pent-up demand of people to exercise those rights, despite the risks involved'.[134]

Tunisian union members and opposition however, did feel this pent-up demand. Bouazizi was not the first who performed the ultimate act of resistance. Just nine months earlier, in a place called Monastir, another fruit vendor expressed his desperateness in exactly the same self-destructive way. And before that there had been severe uprisings in the Gafsa mines for instance. Only this time, when Mohammed Bouazizi set himself on blaze, there were cameras in the form of mobile phones and connection to the Internet, especially the social media. Also, this time the scenery was convenient for stirring up the emotions of the already fed up Tunisian population. Fear was turned into anger. The small Maghreb country inhabits a large group of young, well educated, unemployed next to a poor and struggling rural population that feels neglected by Tunis. Both felt deprived of their basic rights and humiliated by those in power. Unemployment and poverty are not just

---

[134] HRW WR2012 Eric Goldstein, Before the Arab Spring, the unseen thaw, p 37

economic factors, they also lower the self-worth and self-esteem of people, like the Tunisian man told the documentary maker: ones' dignity is worth fighting for.

The story that started the Jasmine Revolution - named after the scenting national flower that is been sold on Tunis' streets to chase the bad odors from the perpetual flow of cars combined with smelly sewage air – was largely made up by opponents of Zine Abedine Ben Ali's repressive regime. According to unionist Lamine Al-Bouazizi (no family of Mohammed) he himself and some members of his group came up with a plan to free the repressed emotions and anger of the Tunisian people[135]. The time was right; the story just needed juicing up. Therefore the activists spread the rumor Mohammed Bouazizi held a university grade, but - like the target group - could not find a job fitting his education. To maintain his mother and siblings he took up fruit selling in the streets. This seemingly small alteration of the truth evoked the anger of many young academic Tunisians frustrated in their search for work and fulfillment.

A second addition to the truth spiced up the rural, foremost conservative community: An unmarried childless female police-agent, the woman who fined Bouazizi for street vendor without a license, would have slapped him in the face. Such act is perceived as the ultimate form of humiliation. Women do not hit men, ever, in the area of Sidi Bouzid, where the drama took place.

A society's prejudices

The above story reveals some very important elements when we discuss human rights and liberties, for however beneficial the uprising may be for the development of a democratic Tunisia - which is still in the drawing phase while writing this - it also shows how destructive a societies' prejudices can be. In this case the policewoman got the blow. She was an easy target, a social suspect. Fayda Hamdi, in her forties, had neither husband nor child. She was the only woman in the police corps of nine. If she were a man, a wife or mother, nobody would have thought about sacrificing her. Now an outraged mass threatened her based on rumors. Nobody came to her defense. Even worse, dictator Ben Ali tried to appease his revolting population by throwing Mrs. Hamdi in jail. Ben Ali together with his much-hated Queen Regent of

---

[135] La Libération, La Révolution de la Gifle, par Christophe Ayad, June 11, 2011

Carthage, Leila Trabelsi, fled the country on January 14, 2011. Mrs. Hamdi stayed in jail for another three months, until April the 19th of the same year.

Women, opponents of repressive regimes, minorities, lesbians and gay, even children parade the catwalk for the abused. They are the first to suffer injustice. Women and children, especially those who belong to a minority, lack sufficient education and health care, even food and potable water in large parts of the world. Extreme poverty leads to even more extreme abuses and inequality.

The civil power

Even if we presume, like the French philosopher Michel Foucault, that systems force human beings into a certain direction, still there will be adventurers who try to manoeuvre as Ulysses did between Scilla (the Market) and Charybdis (the State), searching for free open space where they can experiment with new innovative approaches that once successful will be adopted by the masses. Mind you: these people can be civil servants as well as entrepreneurs or housewives. 'Man is what she or he designs her/himself to be', Existentialists argued. A profound distinction is that a person that dreams, hopes and expects but does not act is not a player/actor, according to Jean Paul Sartre. The advise to individuals is to get their hands in the mud. Deconstruction catalyzes the slack in systems, which is the presentiment of destruction. In the case of Tunisia destruction was burgeoning abundantly. The deconstruction forced by the activists that juiced up Bouazizi's desperate act, left victims. To prevent dramatic and deadly situations it is wise to leave room for dissent and to deconstruct before the destruction phase is entered.

Solving complex global issues such as diminishing biodiversity, poverty, and climate change, starts with the actions of the individual. There is and always will be an avant-garde, frontrunners who run against traffic, who defy the traditions and common sense of the majority. These people design and develop something that was not there before. Anno 2012 the avant-garde finds kindred-spirited people more likely and much faster than ever before through modern day communication, such as Internet and the there present social media that flow straight through vested order, like a rhizome from under the ground, bottom-up. This vested order, as well as regimes, and the larger systems of these orders and regimes, are much easier to disrupt than ever before. This phenomenon makes it even more evident that each change starts with an individual who chooses another direction, for him- or herself, and by doing so, for all other individuals. Even those who do not choose, choose, namely to stay with the masses. Politicians and policymakers are used to choose for others. When those others decide not to comply - even though the government was elected in a free representative democracy - they are not committed. People become committed as soon as they feel compelled through ethics and moral standards of their own.[136] This is what happens when a goal becomes communal, collectively set through equal participation and despite - or because of - individual differences on other subjects, different opinions, religions, tribes or cultural backgrounds. Then something like a Civil Power rises, in between Market and State. This power exists from within, because one person - together with many others - feels the necessity and the appeal of a direction for economic, ecological and socio-cultural developments and the relations between those three capitals. Such is best organized by self-organization, not by hierarchic structures.

The Civil Power differs from a Joint Effort Society, because there are no institutions and it usually concentrates on one issue. People group around this issue - for instance Save the Whales - discuss solutions and share knowledge on, in this case, the Whales and how they can be saved. Apart from the subject, the participants do not need to have much in common. Many times they don't even know each other, they engage through Internet and the social media. After the issue is solved, sank away in time or buried under other pressing involvements, the group dissolves automatically. The Occupy Movement that swept the world in 2011 and was fused by the greed of banks and multinationals - 'We are the 99%' - united people from all backgrounds in a grand protest, can be called a Civil Power. There were no leaders, the whole was done through self-organization and each Occupy had its' own specific goals.[137]

---

[136] Allemaal Winnen, Bakker & Van Empel, Studio nonfiXe, 2012, p. 329/330
[137] The Occupy movement started in the US as Occupy Wall Street on September 17 2011 and was inspired by the Arab Revolution and the Spanish 15 May Movement. Harsh police interventions attracted worldwide attention to the protests. It spread quicker than a virus. Others at different places and in different countries with the same

A Civil Power however can grow into a Joint Effort Society. This happens when institutions rise and the issue is widened, either by more participants or by other subjects that bind the involved.
The Civil Power that develops governance capacity and self-organization becomes institutionalized in some form of democracy.

The rise of the programmed citizen

In the 18th and 19th century European citizens were considered autonomous individuals capable to judge for themselves on societal issues.[138] This has changed in the following era, when professional representatives took over governance. The current politicians and members of parliament have their own opinions on the ideal society. They need a majority of the votes to install these. However in the race to get elected democracy as a way of life is more than often forgotten, as John Keane described.[139]

Professional politicians design laws and regulations to shape society into the desired mall, many times without consulting the minorities. The autonomous citizen has gradually become the programmed citizen. His and her movements are confined in between the crash barriers politicians erected throughout the years to protect them against themselves and to enforce solidarity. Solidarity that is, among fellow countrymen and -women.
In the Netherlands in the 1950's solidarity among Dutch was rather self-evident. The national culture was homogeneous, divided into pillars: Socialists, Christians, and Liberals, to name the three largest. The borders were guarded by customs. If there was a person from outside the country, most of the time this person came from Spain, Italy or perhaps Suriname. Nowadays the borders are porous and distances short, not just because of the EU, but also due to the fact people travel fast and easy and of course due to the Internet. Like-spirited find each other over large geographical distances, they learn from each other, each others' cultures and customs and every community gets soaked with different ideas, words, food, religions and customs. The Dutch

---

feelings of discontent on economic inequalities and other (also societal / ecological) abuses started their own Occupy.
[138] See amongst others Meindert Fennema, De moderne democratie, p. 10
[139] John Keane, Life and death of Democracy, Edition Pocket Books, 2010

population too grew more and more diverse. Today some feel more kinship with others from New York or Tripoli than with their direct neighbour. Besides that the variety inside the Dutch population made solidarity between community members less obvious. Some individuals resisted the diversification of the population fiercely and nationalism grew while solidarity diminished.

Central planning in public interest - such as mutual solidarity - and the concept of a repairable society made it possible for governmental agencies to arrange all kind of things for and on behalf of the citizen, but are at odds with growing self-responsibility and self-reliance of individuals. Citizens that wish to embody such values of individual freedom, responsibility and choice irrevocably collide with governmental agencies that are marked by the complicity within these institutes.

The question invariable rises if a 'lower' control circuit can and may withdraw from the power of a 'higher' control circuit, or for that matter, withdraw from the towering constituent, legislative and executive power of the Nation State. Is the Programmed Citizen allowed to delete a part of the programming and declare him- or herself accountable and free to act? Does parliamentarian democracy offer the space for civil dissent and activism? Just posing these questions leads to new thinking.

The unlimited individual

Mankind, individual men and women, probably aren't greedy as we like to blame our bankers and capitalist companies to be. Greed is not the just word for most of us. We are unlimited. We do not know when to stop gathering things. We have become addicts of material possessions. This is because we value pleasure, even more than joy. Pleasure is quick to achieve, it can be derived from drugs and alcohol for instance… alors, pleasure is the easy way. Pleasure, as defined by Erich Fromm, can be described as instant satisfaction. We can experience pleasure without being active and lively in existence. But when the pleasure is gone, we are no richer, nothing inside us changed. Except maybe for the hangover. Now here is the danger: to kill the hangover, reinstall pleasure. This is where the addiction lays around the corner, waiting with growing satisfaction for yet another individual that looses her or his will (and gradually capability) to act. Societies in a large part of the world have become pleasure addicts, whereas another part of the globe is merely trying to survive. And since pleasure hunting is the current craze, individuals feel they are just and right to follow the pleasure road, as individual characters mirror the features of the community. The others who have never experienced pleasure feel attracted to it. They want to install the program as well. They too will become unlimited consumers of pleasure. This unlimitedness, perhaps even more than greed, is what keeps humanity from changing the path into a more sustainable development.

An addict who wants to quit the habit has an incredible difficult task to perform. Quitting is not about mere will power. It has to do with many a psychological and societal impulse. It has to do with the routines of daily life, with stress and despairs and hopes. Most addicts fall back into their slavery several times. This eats their self-confidence and self-esteem, thus feeding the addiction to instant 'feelgood' and devouring motivation for change.

Motivation loops

Getting rid of an addiction is learning new behaviour, while breaking with the old habit. For starters, one has to be motivated. Psychologist Menno Mennes from Leiden University researched motivation.[140] 'It starts with a fantasy,' he stated. 'During this phase a person is safe. There are no requirements, no tests to the fantasy. The problem begins when someone puts an effort into something. Making an effort turns a person vulnerable, because you either succeed or you fail. It has direct consequences for the self-image, the self-esteem of the person. Many times when someone fails, he or she rationalizes the failure: 'It wasn't my fault, the circumstances…' Or: 'I just didn't have enough time'. According to Mennes a person who fails and rationalizes the failure into something outside him- or herself, loops back, into fantasy. This coping behaviour keeps the harsh reality of failure away, and everything stays in the imagination. It remains like this until reality hits back and the person can no longer deny the failure. He or she will become de-motivated. However things can take another turn if reality is put in a different light and the individual learns that maybe he or she did not try hard enough, and there still is a chance for success. For instance because a teacher encourages the person. This teacher affirms the coping behaviour (the

---

[140] Motivation, Frank van Empel & Caro Sicking, interview with Menno Mennes, 4P, Investors in People, June 2007

fantasy that upholds the self esteem). The result will be that the student tries harder and becomes dedicated to the teacher, while re-adjusting expectations into more realistic ones. Thus increasing the chance to succeed next time.

Menno Mennes: 'Developing internal self-assessment is crucial to motivation. When a person is convinced that immediate success is an unreachable goal, that it is normal to fail before success can be achieved, and he or she just has to try again - harder or different, than this person builds up self-esteem, while adjusting the fantasy. It is a dynamic process,' he added. 'People who are capable of neutralizing reality through their coping behaviour obtain more self-confidence and have more guts.'
Learning new behaviour and getting rid of the addiction for individuals is not so different from how organizations and societies learn. John Kenneth Galbraith spoke of the accommodation of a community that can be broken by avant-garde individuals[141]. The addiction to pleasure seeking instead of joy can be broken the same way.

Triple loop learning
David Kolb described learning as a cyclic process of doing, reflecting, thinking and deciding.[142] Experience is built by doing. We reflect on this experience and think it through. Than we decide what to do next. After the cycle is completed a new circle on a higher level takes place. We are able to test our experience in a new situation. Every time we learn from experiences (feedback) and adjust our behaviour, we reach a higher level of competence. People have to develop such a fashion of learning. In other words we have to learn how to learn, and grow coping behaviour that keeps us motivated. Joop Swieringa and André Wierdsma expanded Kolb's vision on learning into triple loop learning for organizations[143]:

1. Single loop learning: improve the existing, among others by adjusting certain rules;

---

[141] John Kenneth Galbraith, The Nature of Mass Poverty, first printed in 1979 by Harvard University Press, Published in Pelican Books 1980. Reprinted in 1984 and 1987
[142] Experimental Learning, David A. Kolb, 1984
[143] Op weg naar een lerende organisatie, Joop Swieringa & André Wierdsma, 1992

2. Double loop learning: Not just the rules, but the insights behind regulations are discussed. This leads to new things and insights;
3. Triple loop learning: the basic / elementary principles of the organization are open for discussion. Here, real development and change start.

Double and triple loop learning is hardly ever done in traditional organizations. They are applied by learning organizations. We can put the concepts in a matrix that can be applied to organizations, to societies and to individuals as well. As we can conduct from the above, a learning organization / society is most likely filled with learning individuals. And vice verse, triple and double loop learning and motivated individuals are more inclined to form a learning organization or society.

Sustainable development demands knowledge and understanding at least (double loop learning). Triple loop learning organizations, societies and individuals however have an even bigger chance to succeed, because these are prepared to change the paradigm, turn processes, behaviour, technologies and decisionmaking around and upside down, go through the deconstruction phase to find the leverage points for a development towards a higher level. Here principles are the only guidelines and guts is the characteristic that creates the path, by walking it.
The device is Think for oneself! Learn how to form your own opinion on reality and on the systems that form this reality. Dare to be different and to sense. Dare to deconstruct and sense your way through chaos, even if the rest of society does not act the same.

Whistleblowers & change makers
Learning organizations - and societies - cherish whistle blowers and dissidents. They aren't afraid of the 'other sound', because they think they can learn from it. But not all organizations think and act like this. And the bigger and more powerful they are, the more there is to lose, or to protect, the more organizations seem to close up, like oysters hiding the pearl. However these hidden pearls can be pretty black and bad for health.

The power of international corporations is immense. One can even argue that they, instead of governments and international organizations like the UN, rule the world.[144] Just recently it came out that Shell meddled into Nigerian legislation to protect its' oil stream from the Nigerian Delta. It came out through Wikileaks. Now here we hit the difference from the seventies and eighties last century: Internet, social media and a fast growing group of whistleblowers. All scrutinize the conduct of all and go public with the information. Everybody, every government, company and organization is under the magnifying glass of critical watchers. Wikileaks had revealed secret and personal messages and observations of diplomats and governments. But there is more, a growing amount of petition sites clouds the Internet. Every individual person can call upon kindred-spirited to join her in action. The Nigerian women's rights activist and lawyer Nogi Imoukhuede[145] did so to prevent the stoning of a woman called Safiya, who was convicted under Sharia Law for adultery. Mrs. Imoukhuede did it 'the old fashioned way' by spreading emails throughout her connections asking them to forward the message. Today, she just needs to write a petition on Avaaz.org or Change.org et cetera. This means her petition goes way beyond the amount of people she reached with her e-newsletter and the friends of friends that spread the message.

Internet and all that comes with it, is a technological innovation that changed communication. Jeremy Rifkin described how revolutions in communication (due to technical possibilities such as the art of writing and much later, the telephone) became revolutions in social structures. This one changed social structures on global scale. People connect to other people they will never meet, on issue.

Together with this global communication network, that, like every invention, can be used to construct as well as to destruct, to free people

---

[144] Therefore multinationals were among the most targeted by the Occupy Movements.
[145] Mrs. Nogi Imoukhuede is project coordinator of Women's Rights Watch Nigeria and lawyer, dedicated to the empowerment of Nigerian women. Nogi Imoukhuede was one of the human right activists who prevented Safiya Hussaini in Nigeria from being stoned. A Sharia court sentenced her to death, because Safiya was pregnant outside marriage. Her advocates collected support from people all over the world through the Internet. Their political representatives followed duly, turning Safiya's death penalty into an international issue. Safiya survived. Thanks to rising public awareness.

as well as to watch them, a growing amount of world-changers stood up. Every morning new petitions asking 'to take action now!' crowd the email box. On facebook friends and friends of friends post requests to like pages of all kind of charities and companies that do good. Twitter is jam-packed with 140 signs on mothers' health and child birth, on potable water actions, save the tiger, grow a tree, help educate girls, connect against slavery et cetera. In line with this financial organizations sprout to support micro-credits and fund through crowdsourcing. The world is my stage! All I need to force the change I think necessary is access and many, many friends or followers.

Still, a lot of these well-intentioned initiatives die in silence, while the initiators keep busy working day and night to gain cloud. For, how many petitions can one sign? How to find out, what is real and true and what is a scam?

There will be tiredness eventually. On the other hand, the individuals that care for change can commit without too much effort and a new communication infrastructure covers the globe spreading information and knowledge through fast bits and bites. Many participants in this network have jobs in companies that wash their shames green and dress their windows as a masquerade for activities that cannot bear daylight. When employees notice a discrepancy between their virtual activism and daily work the meaning of the daily work vaporizes in relation to the things that 'truly matter'. There are two options on how to deal with the desire for fulfillment: quit the job and go non-profit entirely, or, change the way things are done in business as usual from within. The latter has the advantage of keeping ones own economic independence and not becoming a subject of charity oneself.

Technology & Institutionalization

Introduction
Over 97 percent of humanity's wealth was created in the last 0,01 percent of our history. The wealth explosion was ignited two hundred years ago by the Industrial Revolution. Two types of technology and one actor that combined the technological inventions played a crucial role in the economic growth.

Physical technology (steam engines, micro chips, cell phones) and social technology (ways of organizing, managing and motivating people) are the distinguished co-evolving technologies.
Technical inventions, such as the spinning frame in the 18th century that changed the manufacturing of clothes, made it more suitable and economical to organize labour in large factories, i.e. social technology. The actor that brought both together is business. The capacity of business is just that, organizing people, capital, machines, raw materials and knowledge in one place and turn designs and ideas into tangible products that can be sold making profit.
The magical mix of physical and social technology with the organizational capacity of business allowed the explosion of wealth. It became a system of growth, technology feeds its' own growth.

One of the most remarkable features of physical technology is that each new invention creates both the possibility of, and the need for, more inventions. The invention of the internal combustion engine for example led to the invention of the automobile, which led to the invention of rubber tires[146], windshield wipers, asphalt paving, roadside motels, fast food, toll booths, and drive-through wedding chapels in Las Vegas.[147]

---

[146] This also led to – among others - the devastation of Congo where the rubbertrade caused many victims and still the saying goes: to send someone for rubber, which means to tyrannize. See § 47 White man's primacy. This is only one destructive side of the physical technology that was invented during the Industrial Revolution. This book states that the era brought prosperity and depletion. At first the depletion was confined to the poor and / or excluded, today it is threatening all.
[147] Eric D. Beinhocker, The Origin of Wealth; Evolution, Complexity and the Radical Remaking of Economics, Random House Business Books, 2007, p. 247

What makes one country richer than another is the state of a nation's social technology, or institutionalization. The rule of law, the existence of property rights, a well-organized banking system, economic transparency, a lack of corruption...[148] Social technology is an asset. A country that has sound institutions gets wealthier by the day. Without organizational capacity, a nation falls behind in GDP. Catching up is not easy. 'From a physical perspective it is impossible for poor nations to follow the path of the rich,' E.F. Schumacher wrote in The Age of Plenty.[149] The rich nations have used exorbitant resources. Non-renewable resources. They have not only plundered the poor. They did not only take their oil, rubber, diamonds, and silver, they also withhold them the same possibilities. According to Schumacher 'about one-quarter of the world is immensely rich, and about three-quarters are immensely poor, with very few in between'.[150] This duality, Schumacher stated, is abnormal and unhealthy for both groups, since one has too much and the other too little. Schumacher: 'What exacerbates the problem is that rich societies are perceived as the model which poor societies must follow and aspire to be like. However, if they follow this way through the main entrance they will never arrive where they want to be.'

The poor have to take the backdoor. And that opens to a whole new landscape. 'The real driver of increased productivity,' research proved, 'was changes in how companies were organizing and managing themselves.' The trick is to get organized. Schumacher pleaded for small, human scale production and organization. 'Thus a change of the aims and objectives of society necessitates a change of the production process, the prevailing technology, and the existing organizational framework. The technological change required should move us away from the giantism, infinite complexity, vast expensiveness, and violence to a system which is small, simple, cheap, and nonviolent.'[151]

---

[148] Eric D. Beinhocker, The Origin of Wealth; Evolution, Complexity and the Radical Remaking of Economics, Random House Business Books, 2007, p. 261
[149] E.F. Schumacher, The Age of Plenty, 1993, published in A Survey of Ecological Economics, e.g. Rajaram Krishnan, Island Press, 2007
[150] 1.2 billion people have to survive earning $1 a day. 3 billion people have to live from $2 a day. That means 4.2 billion of the 7 billion can spend a maximum of $2 a day to eat, drink, house & cloth. World Bank, World Development Report, 2000-2001, 22.
[151] E.F. Schumacher, Summary of The Age of Plenty, 1993, published in A Survey of Ecological Economics, e.g. Rajaram Krishnan, Island Press, 2007, p. 343

In this book physical technology is simply called technology, social technology fits into the term institutionalization. Both are in the same solutionfinding cluster. Institutionalization, however, touches governance and decisionmaking directly. The working of institutes such as the European Committee and the United Nations are part of it. Governmental institutions influence the mix of physical and social technology. We discuss governmental institutionalization and business capacity both as together these form the organizational capacity of a society.

Physical technology, especially innovations, can largely contribute to a different society. We will not discuss the latest technical discoveries, building techniques or energy generation. Instead we refer to principles for sustainable innovation, such as formulated by The Natural Step (TNS).[152]

When the rules take over

Next to the physical approach of technology that offers techniques, machines and other smart apparatus, there is the part of the institutions, protocols and procedures. Institutions tend to show slack after a while, they - as if they are living organisms - start to lead their own lives for the benefit of their own survival and lose touch with the objectives they are installed for at the first place. Society needs institutions - such as police, city hall, youth care, parliament et cetera - and civilians tend to develop institutions - such as football clubs, codetermination councils, representative advisory bodies - to stream the actions they believe necessary for a well-functioning society. These institutions follow certain rules and protocols. They objectify their working so personal likes and dislikes are indifferent to the outcome, and corruption is prevented. There are also procedures for efficiency, to prevent the necessity of reinventing fire over and over. For safety and so on.

At some point the rules take over, the objectives are forgotten and the protocol, the procedure or simply the way things are done, gets destructive. At that point the patient is forgotten and becomes the

---

[152] See § Eco principles or go to www.naturalstep.org: 'a network of offices and individual associates that share the same brand, principles and training in strategic sustainable development. [...]Through education, dialogue, coaching and advice The Natural Step provides its partners and clients with deep expertise in sustainability, solutions-oriented innovation and transformational change processes.'

illness, nothing more and nothing less. At that point the 78 year old lady doesn't get the care she needs, for she hasn't reached the age of the demographic yet, which was set on eighty. Then youth care spends fifteen minutes talking to the mother, no more, no less, and fails to look at her children and at the family's specific situation. Then the cleaning of a toilet in a school is set on a strict time limit, no matter how dirty or unhygienic the place is.

Depersonalization is another destructive efficiency tool. Depersonalization turns people into numbers. When they enter an institution they are interviewed using a decision tree. The outcome of the interview is written down in a comprehensive, prescribed manner and sent to another functionary. The latter decides - without actually seeing or hearing the person in question - on the issue. Asylum seekers in the Netherlands are treated this way. When a person has no identification papers, the decision tree branches towards denial. This despite the well-known fact that trafficked people generally have no passport and lie about their country of origin as well as about their trip. These lies usually come forth out of fear for the 'travel agent' and out of shame. Most interviewers deny the signals the person applying for a staying permission gives. The system is not fit for individual approaches. It turns a personal touch into painstaking paperwork for the interviewer and his or her colleagues.

Besides the unrewarding bureaucracy, Dutch migration functionaries have been ordered to follow the 'not unless' principle for admittance and have quota on how many asylum seekers per year they may allow a stay. This system is about quantity, not about the needs of people.

By nature institutes are against dissent and deconstruction, although this is exactly what they need to keep performing constructive and for sustaining a well-functioning democratic society.

Model Holland: institutionalized talks
Hans Blankert, president of the Dutch employers' organization and his counterpart of the employee's association, Lodewijk de Waal, were standing shoulder to shoulder, both smiling confidently and content. They looked like brothers, suited up similarly, red ties as joyful accents. Any outsider might have thought they lived in harmony side by side.

And that is exactly what they wanted the world to believe on September 18, 1997, in Gütersloh, Germany. That day they received the Carl Bertelsmann Prize for the Dutch consultation model, a prize that brought along 300.000 DM[153].

Prime Minister Wim Kok was present as well, just like some members of Parliament and of the SER (Social Economic Council)[154]. It was a feastly gathering. Respectable. Nice. Keeping up appearances.

Flashback

Some 35 years earlier, around 1960, large quantities of natural gas were found in the Netherlands. This natural treasure allowed consumption and government expenditures to grow extensively. The drive for more and bigger should have been corrected by a depreciation of the Dutch currency those days, the guilder. Instead the coin appreciated because of the revenues from gas-field exploitation and gas-exports. With strong guilders import was cheap, but export rates fell. As a consequence unemployment numbers grew. Profit margins were shrinking. The Netherlands became a prime example of a country where growing government spending, a strong currency and rising wage costs had the economy in a stranglehold, known as the Dutch Disease.

The cure for the aching economy was found in the tradition of polderen: talking until a compromise is reached[155]. This time polderen

---

[153] The Euro wasn't installed yet in 1997.

[154] SER is the Sociaal Economische Raad, Social Economic Council. Established in law by the 1950 Industrial Organisation Act (Wet op de bedrijfsorganisatie), the SER is the main advisory body to the Dutch government and the parliament on national and international social and economic policy. The SER is financed by industry and is wholly independent from the government. It represents the interests of trade unions and industry, advising the government (upon request or at its own initiative) on all major social and economic issues.

The SER also has an administrative role. This consists of monitoring commodity and industrial boards, which perform an important role in the Dutch economy. Industrial boards are responsible for representing the interests of particular branches of industry, and are made up of employers' representatives and union representatives. From: About SER

[155] Since the dykes were put up to protect the land from the sea, the Dutch had to cooperate, work together, regardless status, position or wealth, to keep the water out. The term polderen refers to winning land from the sea and became a consultation model about giving some and taking some, ending in an agreement that is a compromise involved parties can live with.

resulted in an agreement between the social partners. Government, employers and unions scaled down consumption together. Wages, salaries and social benefits were voluntarily frozen at the 1982 Wassenaar Agreement. This watershed in Dutch labor relations brought peace at the collective wage bargaining front. It created financial room for investments and strengthened the supply side of the Dutch economy.

The Wassenaar Agreement put the responsibility for collective contracts in the private sector squarely in the hands of the social partners. The Agreement was the beginning of an irreversible shift towards local bargaining, while preserving forms of central coordination. The phrase sometimes used is 'organized decentralization'. The government and the social partners together managed to bring wage costs in line with foreign competitors through national wage restraints in the free market next to cutting and freezing civil service salaries and social benefits. In the next fifteen years, from 1983 to 1997, contract wages in collective agreements rose by a total of 29,5 per cent, an average of less than 2 per cent per annum. The consumer price index, on the other hand, rose over 30 per cent during the same period, i.e. more than 2 per cent per annum. Thanks to the austerity accordance wage costs per unit of product in industry have remained fairly constant over the decades. (By comparison, during the same period wage costs per unit of product in Germany rose an average of 2,5 per cent per annum.) As a consequence business profits recovered, the international competitive position improved, and a more labour-intensive economic progress became possible. Since 1997 the wage moderation went on and labour productivity - one of the cornerstones of long run growth - got a boost.

Dutch global companies (Shell, Unilever, Akzo, DSM) became more efficient and produced continuously expanding amounts of products and services per (full-time) employee and also rising income per capita. This rise in productivity per capita is one cornerstone of the neo-classical growth model of Nobel Prize winner (1987) Robert Solow. The other three cornerstones of the neo-classical growth model are: capital accumulation, population growth and technological progress. According to another Nobel Prize winner in economics (1998), Amartya Sen, the neo-classical economists forgot at least two other very important cornerstones: wellbeing and the freedom that a person actually has 'to do this' or 'to be that'.[156]

Return to Gütersloh

The turnaround of the economy that became known as the Dutch Delight, led to the proud presence of the Dutch social partners who came to collect the German price that memorable September day in Gütersloh, 1997.

The Dutch social partners had a present for their eastern neighbours, a small publication called Model Holland[157]. A booklet all involved had commissioned together and in the end nobody was happy with, because the conclusion of the essay was that employers and unions together ended up 'talking' a substantial number of jobless into the disabled category - thus manipulating the supply-side of the labour market - and by doing so polishing up the employee-numbers of the Netherlands. The parties had different reasons for the reduction of the number of jobless in the graphics. 'The Netherlands have by far the lowest activity rate among older people of all rich Western countries,' is stated in Model Holland. 'It also has a strikingly high number of occupational disabled (one million), a substantial share of whom must be categorized as "disguised unemployed". Labour unions and employers' organizations unanimously have locked the labour market for a substantial part (about 20-25%) of potential labour supply, in order to prevent dumping of low educated, cheap labour.'

These observations hit the core of what is missing in the classical economic approach: the numbers don't match reality. Wellbeing is not considered in economic policy. A multidimensional definition of wellbeing by Stiglitz c.s.[158] included at least the following dimensions simultaneously:

1. Material living standards (income, consumption, wealth);
2. Health;
3. Education;
4. Personal activities, including work;

---

[156] Capability Approach, Amartya Sen and Martha Nussbaum.
[157] Model Holland was written by Frank van Empel, one of the authors of JES!, who at that time was political and economic editor of one of the national newspapers in the Netherlands, NRC Handelsblad.
[158] Joseph E. Stiglitz c.s. Mis-Measuring our lives, The New Press, 2010, p. 15

5. Political voice and governance;
6. Social connections and relationships;
7. Environment (present and future conditions);
8. Insecurity, of an economic as well as a physical nature.'

Another, equally economic approach is that of Professor Thorvaldur Gylfason. Gylfason questioned whether the availability of resources is a curse or a blessing. He also wondered how nation states can deal with natural treasures to benefit the citizens. In his seminar he distinguished several different types of capital that, like plants, are capable of growth at different rates. His classification involved intangible capitals like democracy and freedom. The accumulation of wellbeing determines the success of a region, a country or another (bigger or smaller) community, according to Gylfason.

Determinants of wellbeing[159]:
1. Saving and Investment to build up real capital – physical infrastructure, roads and bridges, factories, machinery, equipment, and such;
2. Education, training, health care, and social security to build up human capital, a better and more productive work force;
3. Exports and imports of goods, services, and capital to build up foreign capital, among other things, to supplement domestic capital;
4. Democracy, freedom, equality, and honesty – that is, absence of corruption – to build up social capital, to strengthen the social fabric, the glue that helps hold the economic system together and keep it in good running order;
5. Economic stability with low inflation to build up financial capital – in other words, liquidity – that lubricates the wheels of the economic system and helps keep it running smoothly;
6. Manufacturing and service industries that permit diversification of the national economy away from excessive reliance on low-skill-intensive primary production, including agriculture, based on natural capital. For example landscapes, managed and/or administered by farmers, may relax people. More in general: spatial quality may

---

[159] Natural Resource Endowment: A Mixed Blessing? Prof. Thorvaldur Gylfason, University of Iceland. Article drawn from the author's lecture at the seminar on Natural Resources, finance and development, Central Bank of Algeria and IMF Institute, Algiers, Nov 2010

enhance the feeling of wellbeing of more people than those who choose to walk and bike in nature, because they have reason to value those activities.

'The freedom to choose our lives,' Sen wrote in The Idea of Justice, 'can make a significant contribution to our wellbeing, but going beyond the perspective of wellbeing, the freedom itself may be seen as important. Being able to reason and choose is a significant aspect of human life.'[160] Measuring wellbeing is difficult, for it doesn't come in numbers and each individual's perception of wellbeing is different. However economic growth evidently is not the indicator for freedom to choose the life we have reason to value. As Sen pointed out in Development as Freedom, it is very likely that a sick person needs a larger income to provide for her or his needs and, due to the sickness, is less likely to earn such than a healthy person. Furthermore, economic growth can very well be obtained at the cost of the wellbeing of labourers or nature's treasures, turning these into a curse. We prefer to talk about progress (economic, ecologic and societal) instead of measuring growth in terms of gross domestic production (GDP). In his book Development as Freedom, Amartya Sen explained the freedom to choose like this: 'As a human being you have the right to live the life that you have reason to value'.[161]

Walking at the supply side
Wealth is based on productivity and productivity is based on technology and organizational capability. As if people don't matter at all, in economic literature the whole economy usually is approached from a pure supply side perspective. The dramatic consequences of the conservative political version of supply side economics of e.g. Ronald Reagan in the USA during the 1980's illustrate this. It strikingly increased inequality.

The first Industrial Revolution too did not happen for the sake of a better life for all people, but occurred - the story goes - in Great Britain at the end of the 18th century, through the application of coal produced, steam powered machinery to mining and the production of textiles, metals and metal products. The steam engine, the locomotive and other

---

[160] Amartya Sen, The Idea of Justice, Penguin Books, 2010, p. 18
[161] Amartya Sen, Development as Freedom, Oxford University Press, 1999, p. 87

technological innovations enabled England to outstrip the rest of the world for a century. From the start of the Industrial Revolution until the late nineteenth century Great Britain's economic leadership remained unchallenged.[162]

Then a second Industrial Revolution rolled over the first one. Investment in production, distribution and management created a modern industrial enterprise that no longer competed primarily on the basis of price, but by improving products, production processes, marketing, purchasing and labour relations. American, German and Dutch companies took over the initiative and left the English behind in smog and dust. These ecological side-effects did not hurt the economy at first, but later, began to bite ferociously.

As it turns out industrialization created growing social hardships. One of which was the result of mass migration of rural poor in search of work to industrial sites, after which they became urban poor, often in even worse conditions. The divide between rich and poor sharpened. Tensions rose and sparked rebellions. It happened first in England, and then, mid 19th century, it happened in France. The USA escaped. While Europe experienced war and destruction, the Americans created a rather new kind of capitalism based on greed and fear. The extravaganza of the Gatsby Years - the roaring twenties - was killed by the Crash of 1929 and the crisis that followed. Business however had learned at least three things from the industrialization[163]:

1. To coordinate and integrate physical facilities (factories, offices, laboratories) and skills in different (supplementary) ways by higher, middle, and lower management;
2. To trigger greed and desires of people, not once but continuously;
3. The importance of moving into growing markets more rapidly and out of declining ones more quickly and effectively than competitors.

In the Netherlands multinationals like Shell, Unilever (both half British), Akzo Nobel and DSM copied the American way of building industrial empires. Productivity growth and wage moderation, both organized in a

---

[162] Micheline R. Ishay, The History of Human Rights, University of California Press, 2004, p.120
[163] Alfred D. Chandler, Jr., Scale and Scope, Harvard University Press, 1994, p. 594

unique framework of consensus building and institutionalized consultation gave the Netherlands a number 10 position in the 2012 ranking of richest countries of the world in terms of GDP per capita. The Dutch play in the same league as the oil kingdoms Qatar, UAE, Norway and Brunei, the financial trade centres Hong Kong and Singapore and paradises for the rich like the US, Luxemburg and Swiss.[164]

A close look at the numbers reveals that the trend that was set by the Wassenaar Agreement in 1982 has been prolonged. In 2012 the Dutch working force above 15 (6,4 million people) had to finance 4,5 million people that were unemployed, sick, disabled or just old.[165] Employment was almost steady over the years, thanks to wage-moderation: real income didn't grow during the last three decades. Income inequality still is relatively small in the Netherlands. Taxes and social security contributions are rather high and progressive.[166]

Productivity in the Netherlands grew continuously and so did wealth. This had a lot to do with the organizational and technological capabilities of the multinationals that characterized the economic structure. Technology had taken over labour that once was done by low skilled workers.

Putting the Dutch social/economic puzzle together leads to the conclusion that productivity and wealth have increased and that this time the wealth indeed trickled down to the point where the working force is just a little larger (1.9 million people) than the group of benefiters. To keep this up, either the Dutch have to support those who are inactive in the job pools to develop knowledge and learn new skills, or investments in innovations will have to grow. Innovations that lead to ecological and social upgrading and create opportunities for all to live the life they have reason to value. For individual wellbeing is not necessarily increased by working a daily job, nor is it by not working. It has to do with fulfillment. Finding the thing to do that gives fulfillment,

---

[164] Forbes, based on OESO-data from 182 countries, 2013
[165] Actualization Dutch economy until 2018, plans of the VVD/PvdA-government included, Central Planning Agency, The Hague, 2012, table 4.2
[166] Actualization Dutch economy until 2018, plans of the VVD/PvdA-government included, Central Planning Agency, The Hague, 2012, table 4.2

leads to wellbeing.

Those who feel they lead the life they have reason to value, contribute almost automatically to a joint effort society. Such contributions vary per person. Like Glenda Jackson stated in the British House of Commons at the memorial of Margaret Thatcher: Society has to understand the individual value of every single human being[167]. Today, nobody will argue the contribution of, let's say, Vincent van Gogh to society, but in his time and age, he was a poor painter economically depending on the benevolence of his brother Theo. Vincent produced without knowing if someone, somewhere, somehow ever wanted to have his work, let alone pay for it. Van Gogh and almost all other artists are used to take a walk at the supply side.

A joint effort society is based on the awareness that not all efforts can be translated to measureable units. The idea of 'making people work' for benefits, is contradictory to the principles of a joint effort society. Recently Dutch communities have obtained the license to think of useful tasks for those who receive an allowance.[168] At a number of city halls they thought of things such as serving coffee to the elder or shovel snow. This type of obligatory work is not creating opportunities, it is putting people down.

Sweden, Denmark, Finland, Iceland and Norway run a similar society as the Netherlands, but the Scandinavian societies have based more of it on laws, formal rules and governmental action. Overall the Dutch way is more informal, a mix of continental and liberal styles and cultures.

These Northern and rich countries are potentially fast developers towards a joint effort society. They have the institutional capacity and a rather highly educated population. These powers can be put to work to create and sustain individual freedoms and ecological and social development. However, taking care of their own will not be enough. The rest of the world needs a piece of the pie too. Than a global

---

[167] Glenda Jackson, MP UK, Tributes to Baroness Thatcher at the House of Commons, April 10, 2013
[168] Dutch local governments are allowed to demand services in return for benefit since 01.01.2012, according to the Law Work and Social Welfare (Wet Werk & Bijstand)

multiplicity of joint effort societies can grow from the bottom up and spread like a rhizome. Where it will end, nobody knows. It is a real life and real time experiment that needs and deserves some sympathy.

The numbers don't match

Over decades rich countries grew richer and learned to use wealth for social improvements. Recently ecology entered reluctantly. Still developments mostly are approached in a compartmentalized way, and the institutions that need to guard the benefits of the welfare state wove long red tapes that hamper progress. There is not a joint effort society to be found in the world yet. Moreover a great part of the economic wealth was obtained breaking the backs of the poor while plundering their resources and destroying environments. Multinationals that behave like good schoolboys at home show completely different faces in other countries.

In support of the rightless and oppressed some international institutions have been founded since WWII. One of them is the International Labour Organisation (ILO). 'The main aims of the ILO are to promote rights at work, encourage decent employment opportunities, enhance social protection and strengthen dialogue on work-related issues.'[169]
Among the key issues are youth employment and social protection. Child labour is one of the great concerns. In terms of a joint effort society, child labour is a cruelty that puts all three solutionfinding clusters squarely in the destruction phase. Here we mainly focus on the institutions that prevent and / or stimulate forced labour and child bondage.

Estimations are that the amount of child labourers is up to 215 million.[170] 'These children, roughly 70 per cent of all "children in employment" (306 million), are classified as child labourers because they are either under the minimum age for work or above that age and engaged in work that poses a threat to their health, safety or morals, or are subject to conditions of forced labour. The number of children in child labour has continued its declining trend, falling by 3 per cent between 2004 and 2008. The corresponding incidence rate declined

---

[169] From the mission statement of the International Labour Organisation (ILO).
[170] Global ILO report 2010, Accelerating Action against Child Labour

from 14.2 per cent to 13.6 per cent.'

In the summary of the same report the ILO wrote: 'However, the critical fight against child labour has to be won in South Asia, where the greatest numbers of child labourers are to be found. Often it is the poverty of policy rather than poverty itself that keeps the mass of children out of school and in child labour.' ILO here expressed faith in policy-makers, which is quite natural to a bureaucratic organization. Policy and legislation can change the lives of people is the underlying assumption. Hence the International Labour Organisation perceived as its' main task to provide labour statistics and standard-setting on statistical indicators[171] in order to support policies and institutions. '[....] Policies and laws responding to child labour need institutions to give them effect, institutions with human and financial resources, political support and specialized technical expertise. Many ways of filling the need for institutional capacity can be seen in modern policy and legislative practice.'[172]

Although a framework of rightful and implemented laws is necessary to protect the individual, in this case a child, from abuse, policy and legislation together are not enough to fill the gap that keeps children from living in bondage. The ILO showed a linear approach to the issue. This behaviour is typical of bureaucratic and technical organizations that rely on data, surveys and equally bureaucratic - and at times autocratic - governments to design 'plans and programs' following certain 'protocols and procedures'. Whatever reality doesn't fit inside the framework is denied as if non-existent.
In The ILO and the informal sector: an institutional history Paul Bangasser described the working patterns of the organization and its' struggle with the informal sector. Starting of in the planning age of the fifties and sixties last century, at some point the ILO had to conclude that 'the numbers didn't match!'[173] Bangasser: 'Even using very favorable assumptions about investment and productivity growth, the number of jobs being created was way short of the projected demand. There were many fewer "modern" jobs than there were people wanting to fill them. Furthermore, many people were often working outside the

---

[171] Global ILO report 2010, Accelerating Action against Child Labour, p. 26
[172] Modern policy and legislative responses to child labour, IPEC 2007, p 92
[173] Paul Bangasser, The ILO and the informal sector: an institutional history, 2000, p 4

framework of their official or planned "work". Some who were officially not "working" at all were in fact economically busy. This came to be called "informal employment", in other words economic activity, which was outside the framework of the official plan. These activities took many forms; "moonlighting" by poorly paid civil servants, cottage industry activities of persons officially "working" as collectivized farmers, or whatever. Urban migration was also a growing phenomenon; and in the urban setting this gulf between the "planned employment" and the visible reality was especially evident. Increasingly large numbers of people were obviously economically active; but what they were doing did not appear in the plan and so, de facto, neither did they.'

This traumatic experience dates from, let's say forty years ago. But still the ILO wrestles to come to terms with informal economics, although it perceives it as central to its' mandate of social justice. When we focus on child labour, much of it takes place in the informal sector, like households, hotels, farms and, even more hidden, in criminal circuits when it concerns trafficked children or children in bondage. Moreover the governing officials that implement a policy should be trustworthy and certainly not corrupt, but this is often not the case. In this matter we refer to Ethics for politicians of Tomorrow as described by Fernando Savater: 'The aim of politics is to organize society the best possible way, so each citizen can choose what is best for her or him. Ethics concerns the use of individual freedom, while politics try to coordinate these personal liberties to the benefit of everybody'.[174]

A joint effort society takes care of the weaker and supports those who cannot support themselves, like children. The problem is, how to support someone without touching his or her dignity and freedom? When combining this question with the natural tendency towards slack that organizations and institutions show, it gets more complicated, for procedures, rules and regulations become self-centred and self-sustaining, overlooking peoples needs. A typical expression for this phenomenon is: 'I can't help it, it is the rule.' Laws are only effective when implemented and enforced for the benefit of a society without interfering with the freedom and dignity of the individual. Not when

[174] Fernando Savater, Het goede leven; Ethiek voor mensen van morgen, Bijleveld, Utrecht, vijfde druk, 1999, p 136/137

they are applied blindfolded without taking the specific situation and unique individual into account, or, worse, when regulations that have lost meaning in the current context are enforced, just for the sake of the regulation, or the regulator.

When we also take into consideration the widespread corruption in developing and underdeveloped countries and the amount of money that goes around in trafficking-country, while politicians and policy-makers end up writing notes, shaking hands, signing covenants that do not emerge from the paper they are written on, it becomes evident that mere policy and legislation will not do the trick.
Amartya Sen wrote in Development as Freedom that [...] 'extreme poverty can make a person a helpless prey in the violation of other kinds of freedom' [next to economic freedom]. Sen named trafficking and slavery and serving in bondage.[175] 'Public policy making is interfering in the systems of society. Great care of the parameters chosen must be taken. We have to make clear what the value judgements are in a field where value judgements cannot be - and should not be - avoided. Indeed public participation in these valuational debates - in explicit or implicit forms - is a crucial part of the exercise of democracy and responsible choice,' the Nobel Prize laureate stated. [...] 'Unnoticed, under-recognized behaviour rules on the way business is conducted in developed capitalist countries,' Sen wrote further on in the same publication, 'are not yet the values in developing markets and countries. One sort of deprivation is the choice of labour.'[176] Mr. Sen could have added the right to being young, education and spare free time to it, in the case of child bondage.

Child for sale
In the Indian region Bihar half the population lives under the poverty line. Especially single mothers endure hardship. Unable to feed their offspring, the only solution appears to sell one of the kids to a trafficker.
The Guardian published on child trafficking in India, August 4 2012: 'Anjura Khatun [mother] knew what to do. The next time the child trafficker came to the village, they agreed a price. A few days later,

---

[175] Amartya Sen, Development as Freedom, Oxford Press 1999, p. 7
[176] Amartya Sen, Development as Freedom, Oxford Press 1999, p. 110 -113

Azam [son] was on a train to Delhi.'[177] Azam was seven years old and had to become the breadwinner of the family. His mother got some money in advance. Since then he worked long days of hard labour in one of Delhi's multiple sweatshops and never got paid again.

Please note the phrase: 'the next time the child trafficker came to town'. It implies that it is rather common to sell your child to a (known!) trafficker as if a kid were a commodity, like fruit or vegetables: 'Child for sale'.

In other words, child labour and child slavery appear to be a cultural accepted phenomenon in the area. However we have to take strong notice of the fact, that whether cultural accepted or not, no parent wants their child to live and be forced to work under such devastating circumstances as Azam was put in. His mother was desperately looking for ways to survive in a neighbourhood where all others had to struggle to stay alive as well. Her personal act of deconstruction, hoping to initiate change for the whole family by selling one child, is doomed to fail because of the larger system she is in. This larger system that includes general acceptance of child labour (and child trade!) is in the destruction mode. Her inability to foresee the dramatic outcome of her decision has to do with her inability to find and change the patterns and structures she is embedded in. Azam's mother felt she did not have the power to change her and her children's lives. She accommodated.

Technology changes behaviour
The above speaks of social technology (institutionalization) and shows where it went wrong. All events together turned out disastrous for a seven year old, and with him for over 200 million other minors. The behaviour that accompanied the social technology was and is just as destructive.

The interesting thing of the complexity we live in, is that attacking destruction can be done from different angles. As the Industrial Revolution showed, physical technology can push change in behaviour and decisionmaking, as well as social technology.
Current technical developments, starting with the worldwide web, have

---

[177] The Guardian / The Observer, India targets the traffickers who sell children into slavery, by Gethin Chamberlain, August 4, 2012

enforced behavioural change. The old saying 'knowledge is power' has been replaced by 'sharing knowledge is power' during the fin de siècle. Growing the 21st century this develops into 'cooperation is power'.

Sharing information, services and products leads to innovative solutions for ecological issues. For example car sharing is a rather recent phenomenon that seemed unthinkable just ten years ago. There was almost a car per person in many Dutch households. This led of course to traffic jams and air pollution next to the use of materials and energy to produce and maintain all these cars. Innovative concepts of car sharing that keep in mind the 'freedom to drive whenever I want to', as well as a choice of the car for the occasion - a large family car or a small city shopper et cetera - are gaining terrain. In the Netherlands the car sharing business grew 25% compared to 2011, already in March 2012. The absolute number of shared cars may not seem impressive, 2649 in total, but these automobiles are used by several drivers, thus replacing at least the double amount[178]. Car sharing is compared to telephones, faxes and facebook: the more the larger the multiplier, Professor Koen Frenken, economist of Innovation and Technological developments, stated[179]. The communication techniques make it possible to have the right types and number of cars available in the neighbourhood. They also support a billing system based on the exact amount of kilometres driven, time of use et cetera. Apart from that the person driving can be traced whenever there are scratches on the car or if it is left behind dirty. The advantage is that a joint car service can provide for new well-maintained vehicles that are less polluting than old cars. When living in a city such as Amsterdam parking ones car can be a curse, not owning one but having a vehicle available at desired times, is quite an attractive option. Besides that, it is cheaper to drive a joint car than to own a car when one doesn't drive more than 12.000 km a year[180].

There are electric cars available as well. The local emissions of an electric car are zero. When it is fuelled by a renewable source, such as wind power, the electric car comes near to the most sustainable transport fashion of these days. This development has gone so fast that

---

[178] Publication Kennisplatform Verkeer en Vervoer, Autodelen aan vooravond van doorbraak, June 2012
[179] Koen Frencken, Daily Trouw, Jongere wil auto wel delen en dat is winst, October 22, 2012
[180] Calculations by Mywheels, 2014

it is no longer perceived as an innovation. But it is. Transport is one of the most destructive sectors in the current society. The number of cars is outgrowing the population growth in percentage, due to rising economies in China and India where people want a car as well. These developing societies can frogleap the Western destructive infrastructure and start to build a more sustainable infrastructure right away. With some help and support of course, of their more rich siblings that already have what the others want. This is of mutual interest, for if all the Chinese people start to drive a conventional car, we the people of the world, will suffer from it, whether we are rich or poor. Although the poor always suffer more.

Resisting change in the company

'Human nature seems to dislike change,' Jerry Yoram Wind and Jeremy Main wrote in Driving Change, 1998. This observation did not withhold them from introducing the 21st century corporation and using 13 dichotomies to distinguish it from the 20th century, classic model. 'It [Driving Change] is based on real-world experience, not academic theory and classroom debate,' Lewis E. Platt, President and CEO of Hewlett-Packard Company, commented upon the book. Wind and Main interviewed top-managers on new characteristics that have emerged since 1985 leading to a list of features of the 20th and 21st century corporation[181]:

Old	New
Goal directed	Vision directed
Price focused	Value focused
Product quality mind-set	Total quality mind-set
Product driven	Consumer driven
Shareholder focused	Stakeholder focused
Finance oriented	Speed oriented
Efficient, stable	Innovative, entrepreneur
Hierarchical	Flat, empowered
Machine based	Information based
Functional	Cross-functional
Rigid, committed	Flexible, learning
Local, regional	Global
Vertical integrated	Networked, interdependent

Wind and Main have examined how companies went about adopting

---

[181] Jerry Yoram Main & Jeremy Wind, Driving Change, Kogan Page, London, 1998, p.4

these new features and what lessons can be learned. They concluded that 'we will have a mix of old and new, the balance varying from company to company'. The authors did not provide insights on the necessary acts for a company to get on the track from Old to New and which were the barriers that needed to be overcome.

Fourteen years later the dichotomies still stand. We even can add one central, overarching dichotomy:

Old: Growth oriented ← → New: Progress oriented

The adage of 21st century business is: economic growth is okay, if business and society together de facto realize zero carbon, no waste, non toxics, and zero poverty. The firm of the 21st century has to be a Zero Hero, a conditio sine qua non for progress.

As a consequence other paradigms need to be replaced. Such as those that lead to transporting containers packed with food, flowers, and used paper around the world. It no longer makes sense and costs a lot of energy and money. That is why local production and consumption are on a comeback.

But whatever may change, change will stay. And since people don't seem to like change, as Wind and Main noticed, and people's institutions appreciate it even less, there will remain friction. 'By far the biggest mistake people make when trying to change organizations,' John P. Kotter wrote in Leading Change[182], 'is to plunge ahead without establishing a high enough sense of urgency in fellow managers and employees. This error is fatal because transformations always fail to achieve their objectives when complacency levels are high.'

Smart individuals usually overestimate how big a change they can force on an organization. They also underestimate how hard it is to drive people out of their comfort zones. Kotter: 'Without a sense of urgency, people won't give that extra effort that is often essential. They won't make needed sacrifices. Instead they cling to the status quo and resist initiatives from above.'

Wind & Main explained that corporations are much like all other organizations throughout history. Medieval guilds would expel a

---

[182] Kotter, J.P., Leading Change, Harvard Business School Press, 1996

member who dared to experiment with the traditional way things were done. In ancient Egypt physicians were trained to perform exact procedures, each in only one way. Egyptian artists learned there was only one way to paint a crocodile or a person. Kotter: 'The key lies in understanding why organizations resist needed change, what exactly is the multistage process that can overcome destructive inertia, and, most of all, how the leadership that is required to drive that process in a socially healthy way means more than good management.'[183]

One thing is for sure: we cannot do without organizations, no matter how conservative they are. 'Individuals alone never have all the assets needed to overcome tradition and inertia except in very small organizations,' Kotter stated. Besides urgency, he argued, at least two other conditions are necessary for major change: a strong guiding team and a sensible vision. Here we like to add, a sensible shared vision. To avoid resistance and to be able to take all relevant aspects into account, it is beneficial to engage all stakeholders in the process of designing a vision. More precisely: the vision is already there in what binds the stakeholders. One just has to find the right formulation.

The above goes for desired change inside a company, top-down, when profits fall and the organization feels the need to reset itself for survival. In the destruction phase the consumers walked away, talented employees quit and started to work for the competition or, started their own enterprise. Such trends can change the course of a multinational into a more truly sustainable fashion of operating. Usually the line of command changes with this new strategy, leaving more room for bottom-up initiatives for the talented workers.

Multinationals like Shell had to find new concepts for its' operations after the Brent Spar sank and the world witnessed oil spill killing seabirds and fish. Companies such as Nike had to convert to different production methods after the scandal of child labourers came to light and the public turned away from the shoe manufacturer.
These two events have a few things in common:

1. The behemoths (and with them all other big business) had no

---

[183] Leading Change, John P. Kotter, Harvard Business School Press, 1996 p 16

internal ethical objections in doing business at the cost of nature or of dependent, vulnerable human beings. They just wanted to produce as cheap as possible and sell as much and expensive as they could in order to maximize profits and satisfy their shareholders. The goal for business is profit, profit, profit. And the cost counted is cost counted in terms of currency, not in terms of societal or ecological losses;

2. Public opinion - image - changed production methods and drove the companies to what is now called: social corporate responsibility, out of fear of losing business;
3. Public opinion wouldn't have changed if the public had been unaware of the ecological and social disasters caused by unscrupulous profit chasers.

Royal Dutch Shell and Nike, and with them numerous other competitors for market share and low cost production, had to change to stay in business.

But the change came from the outside, consumers voted with their feet and sales dropped. The competition that performed business in the same manner saw they had it coming too and tried to stay ahead of reputation damage by publicly announcing they went about in a different, more ethical way. Most of it though was window dressing and recently this term got a 21st century brother: green washing.

Energize the world
Change in the company's core seemed inevitable to Amory Lovins. In the preface of the Rocky Mountain Institute's publication Reinventing Fire he put forward five questions to business leaders[184]:

1. How would your business work without oil, on just a few weeks' or days' notice?
2. What would your firm do if the lights didn't turn on tomorrow or next year?
3. Do you understand the implications of vastly higher energy prices and price volatility for your company, your customers, and your suppliers?
4. How can you win by eliminating your energy operating costs -before

---

[184] Reinventing Fire, bold business solutions for the new energy era, by Amory Lovins and Rocky Mountain Institute, Chelsea Green Publishing, 2011, Preface p. xiii

your competitors do?
5. What pieces of the multi-trillion-dollar new energy economy do you intend to get?

Lovins words were dedicated to vested companies in the 'old economy', and not yet shifted towards the idea of a joint effort society that is about social entrepreneurship and cooperation where profit and planet underpin people. Lovins spoke of competition and about being the first one to find new business, markets or energy. His words were important though for they might very well sound through in the ears and minds of some of the world's largest multinationals and change business as usual into a (more) sustainable, less energy devouring and polluting way of doing business. There is a lot to gain at power plants, oil drilling islands, in the petrochemical industry, the steel and metal sector et cetera.

Reinventing Fire centres around two big stories of our time, oil and electricity and the sectors where the most is to be gained through efficiency and change: industry, transportation and building.
The RMI set goals for each sector, explained the business opportunities, showed the bottom line, pointed at sectors that can profit and wrote down policy enablers.

For example on transportation[185]
>The Goal. In 2050, superefficient autos, trucks, and planes, far more productively used, need three-fourths less fuel and no oil and have less life-cycle cost than the vehicles of today. Yet they provide 90% more automobile-miles, 118% more truck-miles, and 61% more airplane seat-miles with uncompromised convenience, safety and performance.
>The Business opportunity. Radical efficiency enables alternative propulsion and fuels, transforming vehicle manufacturing for break-through competitive advantage, while customers save money and mobility options expand. Society eliminates oil dependence, reducing many security and business risks
>The Bottom Line. Oil not needed saves $3.8 trillion (in 2010 net preset value)
>Business sectors that can profit. Vehicle manufacturers and suppliers, chemical and electronics industries, fleet operators, entrepreneurs, real-

---

[185] Reinventing Fire, bold business solutions for the new energy era, by Amory Lovins and Rocky Mountain Institute, Chelsea Green Publishing, 2011, Chapter 2 Highlights

estate developers, electric utilities, farmers and foresters.

>Policy enablers. Innovative state, regional, or federal policies can remove barriers to buying superefficient vehicles and using them in smarter ways – without new federal taxes, subsidies, mandates or laws (with a minor exception about truck weight limits).

Content: a Joint Effort Society

Introduction

Context and concept together give birth to meaning, which is the content, the 'beef' so to say. Content makes something real and valuable. The theory of ecolution can lead towards a higher ecological, economic, socio-cultural and psychological level of society and all those who live in it. A society decides just as much how the people in it behave, as the individual influences the developments of a society. Successes and failures, trials and errors and what we learn from these experiences, shape us and our surroundings. At the individual level all men and women want to lead a meaningful and productive life. In this aspect there is no difference between the CEO of a multinational and a mother in Tunis. What somebody perceives as meaningful is up to her- or himself. However the access a person has to developing his or her capabilities, the freedoms a person has, to participate in society, to speak out loud, to choose a way of living, to move around etcetera, are essential for his or her fulfillment and ability to lead a meaningful life. Amartya Sen put it like this: all people have the right 'to live the life they have reason to value'. This concept immediately calls on to all kind of dichotomies that need to be solved by one person in relation to other persons and to the environment. It calls for dialogue and discussion and it calls for manners to join opposites. That is what this chapter, the Content is about.

No equilibrium

Sustainable development cannot be constructed, because of the complexity of systems, structures, processes and cultures. One can impossibly oversee the consequences of all intentional or un-intentional interventions in nature or in society. The only way forward is to learn how to deal with uncertainties, insecurities, complexity and chaos, while learning to adapt to changing challenges. It resembles nursing an ecological garden, where space is preserved for the 'wild' in nature. This is a natural process of adapting, bottom up, to a game of power and counter power, which is organic, flexible, dynamic, cyclical and evolving. It is everything but mechanical and linear. Straight lines do not exist in nature.

Ecologists speak of wild systems when an ecosystem is in full range and fully functioning, when an ecosystem contains all the elements it possibly can obtain. Thus when it is complete.

In theory economy, ecology and society may be brought in a state of balance by the market mechanism and turn society complete, but in practice this state of equilibrium has never been, and will never be, realized.

One reason is the wildness[186]. The relations between economic entities like consumption, investment, import, and gross national product, in almost all neo-classical models (mathematical constructions of a supposed reality) are linear and sequential, while in reality they are non-linear and simultaneous. So, the World we think we see in our models and derive from our data is not the real World. That makes any forecast tricky. Policy and strategy built on such models are founded on quicksand.

Another reason why the equilibrium cannot be realized by the market mechanism is globalization, which is a kind of World War III between economic empires. For the benefit of the shareholders of the global company, natural resources in faraway countries are plundered and transported over long distances to so-called cheap labour countries in order to become sexy products that are designed in Western boutiques, marketed world wide via numerous multi media channels and delivered by UPS or TNT.

This leads to the third reason why equilibriums are never found; they are not sought for. Producing and collecting goods has become an end in itself, instead of a means. The consequence is that supply and demand are created artificially, and continuously are being boosted for the satisfaction (i.e. profit) of the producer.

Reality follows the clues of nature
There are many concepts at our disposal or waiting on the side wing to be discovered, created or activated. They can be used to give human behaviour, technology, institutions or the way we make decisions a boost in order to solve a problem or to improve the quality of

---

[186] The wilderness of deconstruction needs a little elaboration, as wilderness or the wild has a special meaning in this context. Wild implies the pure, uncultivated, untamed, disordered, free, spontaneous, unaffected, in humans and animals.

something in a natural way. Managers, directors, educators, and tutors, who are inclined to impatience, very easily get off road. They know what they want. They exactly have in mind how their commands, instructions or suggestions are meant to work out, but they communicate the wrong way - from the top down - or they simply go too fast for the multitude. 'In a natural way' is like 'go with the flow'. Sometimes one has to wait for someone to come along or for something to happen. Then all of a sudden things that seemed frozen, start to burgeon. Nobody knows what the frozen have been waiting for, but when it happens everybody knows for sure this is ít. Or, in the words of the 17th century Dutch philosopher Benedict de Spinoza: 'Reality follows the clues of nature, which only can be felt by intuition, the most reliable source of knowledge'.

Already in 1677 the greatest Dutch philosopher of all times offered 'a framework for better understanding'. 'All things which come to pass,' Spinoza wrote, 'come to pass according to the eternal order and fixed laws of nature.' However, this nature is so complex that our brains run short of capacity to understand its workings. Spinoza: 'Human weakness cannot attain to this order in its own thoughts, but meanwhile man conceives a human character much more stable than his own, and sees that there is no reason why he should not himself acquire such a character.'[187] This higher pitch of perfection was Spinoza's drive and largest ambition. More than three centuries later mankind is still trying to get to it.

The concept of brotherhood
The European Union is a good example of cooperation rooted in a simple insight: countries are better off when they work together than when at war with each other. Large areas of Europe previously have been brought under one banner by empires built on force, such as the Roman Empire and Nazi Germany. Julius Caesar, Napoleon, Bismarck and Hitler were Lords of War, not of Consultation. The result: destruction.

Already before 1914-1918 (World War I) many artists, writers and thinkers, among which the 19th writer and statesman Victor Hugo

---

[187] Benedict de Spinoza, On the Improvement of Understanding, 1677

(1802-1885), turned to the idea of some form of unified Europe. Hugo spoke of brotherhood as a weapon against war at the Peace Congress in Paris in 1849: 'A day will come when your arms will fall even from your hands! A day will come when war will seem as absurd and impossible between Paris and London, between Petersburg and Berlin, between Vienna and Turin, as it would be impossible and would seem absurd today between Rouen and Amiens, between Boston and Philadelphia. A day will come when you France, you Russia, you Italy, you England, you Germany, you all, nations of the continent, without losing your distinct qualities and your glorious individuality, will be merged closely within a superior unit and you will form the European brotherhood, just as Normandy, Brittany, Burgundy, Lorraine, Alsace, all our provinces are merged together in France. A day will come when the only fields of battle will be markets opening up to trade and minds opening up to ideas. A day will come when the bullets and the bombs will be replaced by votes, by the universal suffrage of the peoples, by the venerable arbitration of a great sovereign senate which will be to Europe what this parliament is to England, what this diet is to Germany, what this legislative assembly is to France. A day will come when we will display cannon in museums just as we display instruments of torture today, and are amazed that such things could ever have been possible.'[188]

The Fraternity that was Hugo's revenge would take almost exactly a century and two world wars. During those hundred years the non-Western world was screwed up as well. The scramble for Africa that led to the killing of millions and to the disruption of the natural course of whole societies went full steam ahead. Hungry for slaves, for raw materials, for rubber, gold, diamonds and coals the West divided the rest of the world at the Berlin Conference. Borders were drawn on a map, literally with a red pencil. A part for England, some for France, a little bit for the Netherlands, and a piece for Portugal, here's a few hectares for Spain, leaving forest for Belgium et cetera.[189] The white race dictated other peoples how to live (ethically, religiously, juridical, morally) to the extent of which language to speak in the colonies.

Is the world wiser now in the 21st century? Erich Fromm[190] described

---

[188] My Revenge is Fraternity, Victor Hugo, Peace Congress, Paris, 1849
[189] See § White man's primacy
[190] Een kwestie van hebben of zijn, grondslagen voor een nieuwe levensoriëntatie in de consumptiemaatschappij, Erich Fromm, Bijleveld, 3e druk, 1987

the direct coherence between the average individual and the socio-economic structures of the society surrounding this individual. The result of this reciprocity is what Fromm calls social character. The socio-economic fabric of a society shapes the social character of its' individual members so compulsively, that these individuals actually WANT to do what society TELLS them to do. These two systems, the individual and the collective, influence each other continuously. To be able to change course from a destructive (resource devouring, social inacceptable gaps) society into a constructive society, individuals and the whole need to change behaviour. Jean Paul Sartre defined an individual by his or her deeds. Action determines the person. And if necessary, the individual has to rise above the system, to be able to change the system.

History teaches how hard this is. People form communities they want to participate in. These communities have written and unwritten rules, through religious and secular legislation as well as the way things are thought off and done (traditions, socio-cultural values and norms). An individual growing up in a certain environment is formed according to the orientation frame of these surroundings. One cannot think or be like someone who has a different background, talents, capabilities and fears. I will always be me and see the world from my perspective. You will always be you and perceive the world from your perspectives. One can build character, change paradigms, but one cannot change temperament neither background, which is past experience and cultural heritage. Many people who have been deprived of the comfort or luxury they believe others have, strive for this, since society perceives the apparent rich as successful and with success, status enters. That is one of the reasons why the poor, when they leave poverty, start to long for the perqs of the rich. The populations of developing countries like China and Brazil develop a taste for cars, television sets, fast food et cetera. They are apparently oblivious to the pollution, obesity and other welfare diseases that come with it.

They tell the West they are entitled to material luxury (and its' diseases and addictions), just like the Western population has been. In a sense they are right, why should perquisites be confined to the 'happy' few? The answer has to do with the stage of awareness people have reached.

There are five stages of awareness:
1. Existing without the species knowing it exists – like rocks, water etc
2. Staying alive - plants
3. Consciousness - animals
4. Awareness - people
5. Self-awareness - people

Awareness is being conscious and knowing that you are. Therefore awareness can grow, and evolve, through active exercising, into self-awareness. A person that is aware of things (relations, motivations or patterns) is able to change those. Once that person becomes self-aware, s/he can change his/her own behaviour. He or she can put their mind to changing the reality they live.

'More, bigger & faster' has been proven unsustainable. The status that comes with it is a false perception of happiness. For a long time people have seen (more and more, bigger and bigger) property as security and the expression of success. But the more you have, to more you have to hold on to. The more you will have to protect. There is some level of maximum on possessions, when it comes to happiness and safety. Beyond that level the property takes over and the person becomes his or her properties' slave. Erich Fromm distinguished between To Be and To Have. When a society grants To be over To have, more individuals will move over to Being. To have than becomes rather pitiful. Such a society values wellbeing, happiness and cooperation above wealth and competition. In this light Fromm described the contours of a new human being. He argued that the only way for mankind to escape catastrophe - in spiritual-cultural and economic way - is when a profound change of character is accomplished: To Have must become To Be. According to Fromm this is possible if:

• We suffer, plus we are aware of our suffering;
• We understand the origin of our misery;
• We acknowledge that we can overcome the misery;
• We accept that, to overcome the suffering, we will have to live our lives according to certain principles and guidelines and change our current behaviours.[191]

---

[191] Een kwestie van hebben of zijn, grondslagen voor een nieuwe levensoriëntatie in de consumptiemaatschappij, Erich Fromm, Bijleveld, 3e druk, 1987, p 166

Still the societal model in which Fromm lived, and we are still living in, has been built on the principle To Have. Most of our laws and institutes are designed to protect property. The old paradigm is that property means independency and thus security and therefore freedom. The odd situation is that the security society feels is necessary to protect property and thus independence and individual freedom, that exactly this security is a threat to individual freedom.

Economics how it should be

The mainstream answer to muffle criticism on social and ecological destruction by upcoming economies is, like Dambisha Moyo stated, 'easy for the rich to say we can't have what they have. We need the fossil fuel technologies for our struggling economies. We are hungry.' This is a shortsighted vision on both development and on human needs. Manfred Max-Neef, Chilean economist, has a different interpretation of poverty, more in line with the views of Amartya Sen from India and in the same spirit as the philosophies of E.F. Schumacher and Erich Fromm.

Five postulates and one fundamental value principle underpin Max-Neef's vision[192]:
1. The economy has to serve the people and not the people the economy;
2. Development is about people and not about objects;
3. Growth is not the same as development and development does not necessarily require growth;
4. No economy is possible in the absence of eco-systems services;
5. The economy is a sub-system of a larger finite system in the biosphere, hence permanent growth is impossible.

The fundamental value principle sounds like this: Nothing can be more important than life - no economic interest, under no circumstance can be above the preference of life.

Max-Neef determined nine fundamental human needs that are interrelated and interactive, with the exception of the first: staying

---

[192] Manfred Max-Neef, Barefoot Economics part 2, Economy how it should be, youtube

alive[193]:

1. Subsistence;
2. Protection;
3. Affection;
4. Understanding;
5. Participation;
6. Leisure;
7. Creation;
8. Identity;
9. Freedom.

He defined them as axiological, value related. These fundamental needs interact with existential needs of Being, Having, Doing and Interacting. Max-Neef, like the theory of ecolution, used a matrix to visualize the interconnectedness.

The proclaimed needs are consistent through cultures and time, according to the Chilean economist. A society's character can be revealed by the quality and quantity of the satisfiers it chooses, but the fundamental human needs stay. There is no hierarchy, no linearity. They form a network of equals. Max-Neef argued: 'Any fundamental human need that is not adequately satisfied reveals a human poverty.' Education for example can be seen a satisfier of (among others) understanding. Books - which are produced goods in the economy - are the attributes. A predominant economical approach is harmful. One glance at the list is enough to understand that neo-classical economics is not the answer to create a future. We are producing products as an end, not as a means for the benefit of life. Manfred Max-Neef described the crisis of his native continent Latin America in 1986 as the crisis of Utopia. 'The most serious manifestation of the crisis is that we lost our capacity to dream.' He wrote about a state of depression and feeling inferior, fear and anxiety, cynicism, over-excessive individualism, a sense of defeat, demobilization and the loss of will. He described accommodation, but refused to surrender and fought by designing a mental framework that has been put to practice in several places in South America. The matrices of Max-Neef are divided in

---

[193] Based on Manfred Max-Neef, Real-Life Economics: Understanding Wealth Creation, ed. Paul Ekins & Manfred Max-Neef, Routledge, London, 1992, download

negative and positive observations through the categorization of satisfiers. Four exogenous satisfiers are classified as violators, pseudo-satisfiers, inhibiting satisfiers and singular satisfiers[194]. The latter influences just one need and therefore is assigned as neutral. The other three are destructive and lead to the crisis of Utopia, to the attitude of accommodation. The endogenous satisfier, the fifth in the row, is called the synergetic satisfier. This type of satisfier improves multiple of the nine fundamental needs and ameliorates self-reliance of a community. A concept that comes close to selforganization of a control-circuit that can be a local community, region or nation state.

The beautiful thing of the fundamental human needs is that they can lead to potentiality as well (as to deprivation). Again it starts with awareness and the will to succeed. Once a community is aware of the nature of its' satisfiers, it can choose to use the needs as a motor. Need can become a resource. This reminds of post-traumatic growth some people are capable of.

In our (the authors of this book) practice we have met victims of women trafficking who escaped from slavery and were able to turn the traumatic experience of their past into a power that energizes not only their own self but also others. They have become experience-experts and supportive of others. These women recognize in the blink of an eye who is in bondage and how she can be rescued. They know the walk and talk and, they act in empathy with understanding. Their curse has become a resource a.k.a. a saving ability for others and at the same time an empowering force from deep inside.

The joint effort society: a model for peace & progress
Of all three P's - People, Planet, Profit[195] - the P of People stayed in the niche most of the time. The economy has been dominant overall. The ecology counts as far as it impairs economic growth. People are the most neglected species. In the world today billions starve. People

---

[194] A violator for example is arms race that impairs, among others, the need Freedom / a pseudo-satisfier is a false sensation of satisfying / an inhibiting satisfier for, among others, Freedom is paternalism / a singular satisfier satisfies one need and is neutral to all others. Max-Neef defined the singular satisfier as a characteristic of development and cooperation programmes. A synergetic satisfier such as self-management production or direct democracy stimulates, among others, Freedom.
[195] These three P's form the bottom line for economic developments. Cannibals with Forks, John Elkington.

struggle for survival in filthy mines in South Africa, get screwed for oil in Nigeria, are denied fertile soil in Ethiopia, are sold as slaves, denied asylum, excluded and banned from the free and wealthy life that is so apparent for the greater part of their Western siblings. Mankind is the biggest destroyer of man. The father of contemporary economics, Adam Smith, claimed that altruism is a human characteristic as well as self-centredness. Humans are the dominant species, because they are able to work together, share and learn accumulative. It worked in a way for Europe for more than sixty years. The European Union at least tried to level large income disparities through allocation of (financial) means and knowledge dissemination.

This book spoke of capabilities, needs and wellbeing. It included context, concept and content, and approaches these through three solutionfinding clusters - behaviour, technology / institutionalization, decisionmaking - that, together with three phases - destruction, deconstruction, construction - can be put inside a matrix to measure, direct and evaluate sustainable development as it is meant by ecolution.

The vision of a community that is capable of creating solutions together can be referred to as governance capacity. When a region, municipality or other group of people has such a capacity and continuously uses and applies it, it becomes a joint effort society (JES). Its' attractiveness lies in the characteristic that everybody wins compared to the situation they are in now.
The economy is embedded in the ecology. This assumption is based on accumulative evidence that the Earth's supplies are running short and mankind faces a mutual enemy: the destitution of the planet we live on. Since human beings are experts in cooperating once they see the value of working together, and geniuses in finding solutions, but on the other side are change-avert and self-centred, a society needs checks and balances, next to a shared vision, to function well. The economy provided for checks and balances in the Western countries for a long time, but at great costs. Economists spent their intellectual capacities, their time and energy on describing and prescribing ways to stimulate economic growth and how to share the profits. The economic systems have gone completely out of control. The economy has become an end in itself instead of a means for a good life.

The self-producing individual

Living organisms - man in particular - are autopoietic. Auto meaning Self and Poietin is Produce. Self-producing, making one self.[196] The self-producing man or woman seems not to be inclined to change behaviour unless he or she gets into trouble (a crisis). A profound deconstruction that opens systems and networks (inside and around a person) is necessary.

The main religions have divergence in common. They stimulate pro- and contra movements. People think something is good or it is bad. For a long long time the communis opinio has been that systems are based on selection. Survival of the fittest. This battle for the Earth between organisms has been the dominant survival strategy until recently. For where affluence lives, one can afford competition, but once scarcity enters so obviously, cooperation leads to more for each.

A new stream arose between Market and State. This civil power and its tributaries drain into ethics and moral principles. It consists of streams and movements such as:

- Primacy of the region
- Commons
- Arising of new co operations
- European Model
- Existentialism as Motivator

In his book Over het Existentialisme Jean Paul Sartre broke a lance for the engaged individual who chooses to act and by doing so invites others to back up words with actions. Sartre: 'A human is involved in life. He leaves traces and that is all. There is nothing more out there. This may be a discomforting thought for those whose life is not a success. On the other side, this notion forces people to realize that reality is the only thing that counts. Dreams, expectations and hopes guarantee nothing more than the definition of man as a discomfiture, a dream that did not come true. Expectations, dreams and hopes define women and men in a negative way.'

---

[196] Marcel van Herpen, Ecologisch Verantwoord Onderwijs, artikel uit reeks van vier, ter gelegenheid van het jubileumjaar 2005-2006, dertig jaar ErvaringsGericht Onderwijs.

Get up, stand up and act, Sartre shouted in the call for profound social ethics that people feel committed to and act upon. This makes law and order to enforce rules almost redundant. The primacy of the individual will overarch the primacy of the state. The power of governments then reduces to a negative power - only to mediate in conflicts between the freedom of one versus the freedom of the other.

Most of the time developments towards social change appear in smaller communities - networks, peer-to-peer groups. Regional and local governments that realize this obtain a new raison-d'être. They can bind people, stimulate, coach, mediate, and facilitate developments that sprout from the community. Local and regional governments can become the brokers to guide bottom-up initiatives, directs, bundles and connects these with a coordinating policy by the state. Regional governments are in the right position to provoke ecolution, to guide through the wilderness of deconstruction and co-instigate the transition from a destructive man to a constructive, active citizen. And vice-verse the active and aware citizen creates, sustains and scrutinizes constructive governance, as well as cooperative institutes and healthy technologies.

Sustainable environment and peace
A new challenge to democracy is found in the ecological issues and troubles that have become clearly visible in today's world. The issues concern climate change, diminishing biodiversity, extreme poverty, depletion of fossil fuels and other natural resources. Who in democracy takes care of nature? Most of these issues are not confined within the borders of one nation state, nor to one generation. They call for a global approach. The EU model can provide a part of the answer, since it overarches different states[197]. It is what John Keane called 'a multi-layered political community' and 'an experiment in regional integration'.[198] Some frontiers are natural, set by a river, sea or chain of mountains, but many a nation state is conceived through wars and conquests, dividing tribes as well as uniting different ones. Apart from this, nation states tend to compete with each other and, as Donald Rumsfeld stated: 'In difficult situations, governments do not discuss

---

[197] 27 memberstates in September 2012, along with treaties with bordering countries.
[198] Life and Death of Democracy, John Keane, First published by Simon & Schuster UK Ltd, 2009, Edition Pocket Books 2010, p. xxv

pressing matters'.[199] Regions however do not feel the same urge to compete with other regions in different countries. By allowing regions to cooperate on global issues with local means and involvement, the EU pulls the angle out of national politics and its' reluctance to discuss pressing matters. When five regions cooperate on green renewable energy on their own territory, they are not competitors, but learn from each other's successes and mistakes.

It worked in the POWER program on Low Carbon Economies[200]. The regions Andalucia, Emilia-Romagna, Malopolska, Noord-Brabant, South-East England, Stockholm and Tallinn cooperated on several energy issues from biomass to sustainable transportation and continued their cooperation in other EU Programs, due to the successes and joint accumulative learning the involved experienced and valued. From the foreword of the Power publication: 'Europe is a continent of regions. Regions often have more ability to find common ground on community matters then nations. There are several reasons for this, among which the difference of scale that determines the nature of governance. Regions are closer to the citizen than the nation is. Moreover, competitive and sovereign issues play a far less important role between, let us say, Cadiz and Noord-Brabant than between the government of Spain and that of the Netherlands. Especially the trend of decisionmaking closer to the base due to the rise of a mature, independent and worldwide connected citizen, a trend, which is enabled by communication innovations like Google, facebook and twitter, leads to new steering methods coming into fashion.'

Permissive consent: the general direction is clear
The European Union has its foundations in a special kind of consent, called 'permissive consent'. The Commissioners in Brussels are supposed to act in line with the intentions of the EU in all its aspects. So long as nobody peeps the commissioners can do what they think is right. The general direction is clear. Every seven years a 1.000 billion euro EU-budget is authorized, which is a painstakingly process involving all national leaders and interests. After the authorization the

---

[199] Secretary of Defense of the US Donald Rumsfeld at a Press Conference on October 7, 2001. CNN.
[200] Power Essays, Provincie Noord-Brabant, Frank van Empel & Caro Sicking, Studio nonfiXe, 2011. Download

show can move on without having to ask permission of each member state for every decision. Concrete actions take place around the same long-term trend. This model keeps decisionmaking in a large body as the EU - 27 collaborating nation states, ca. 500 million people -flexible, dynamic and future oriented.

The art of consultation[201]

Of all the ways of coming up with solutions to steer today's society collaboration appears the most convenient one, since top-down command doesn't work for a community of self-producing individuals and does not fit into the joint effort society. For collaboration consensus or consent is possible, but not a must. Dissent is encouraged. Disagreement is respected. Central to all forms of collaboration is the presence of shared interest and power.

Each situation, issue or problem is different from all others. It is more or less authentic and so are all solutions. To find the answers, or to create these, one will have to be some kind of artist and will have to accept that there are no rules in art and architecture, but there are some principles, capacities, capabilities, and shared visions.

The art of consultation contains the capacity to use the energy and competence of the group in several ways. It is a bottom-up process. The best results come when no one cares about who gets the credits. There is no room for private agendas, preconceived ideas and ulterior motives here. The way to achieve that is to share a common vision of what has to be accomplished.[202] Consultation is a series of attitudes or behaviours of which Me = We is one. One agreement for instance is that everybody is expected to give the fullest attention to the one who is speaking. When each person concentrates on what is being said instead of thinking about his or her own statements, ideas have the best developing opportunities.

---

[201] Based on John Kolstoe, Developing Genius, George Ronald Publisher Ltd, UK, 1995
[202] John Kolstoe, Developing Genius, Georg Ronald Publisher Ltd,. 1995, p. 33

My idea →   ◎   → Shared vision

The concepts 'My idea' and 'Shared Vision' are opposed and interdependent at the same time. They are abolished in a concept of a higher order: 'Me = We'.
A young child is completely egocentric. It simply cannot think of itself as someone with an identity that differs from those of other people. It believes itself the centre of the universe. While growing up the separation between the I and the others gradually becomes evident for the child. Still the I is the starting point from which the surrounding world is viewed. Throughout the years ego-centeredness shrinks and (self-)awareness rises. Me can become We. In society, alike in a person, such processes take a lot of time.

The Mutual Gains Approach
The Mutual Gains Approach (MGA) aims at solutions approved by as many stakeholders as possible. It is based on mutual understanding and on the willpower to succeed. Negotiations about mutual gains presuppose that people have a consensus-orientated attitude. 'A package deal almost always is possible,' Lawrence E. (Larry) Susskind, who laid the foundations for this approach, stated. Together with associates of the Consensus Building Institute in Cambridge (USA) Susskind wrote The Consensus Building Handbook, a comprehensive (1145 pages) guide for reaching agreement. The authors claimed that consensus building works best when four preconditions are met:

1. Group participants must tap the right kind of facilitation or mediation assistance;
2. Groups need to formalize their commitment to consensus building by adopting written 'ground rules' or bylaws, behavioural & procedural guidelines, etc;
3. Sufficient time for groups to build their capacity to work this way;
4. A clear map, outlining how to build consensus.

The handbook sought to provide that map, including ground rules and guidelines. Susskind offered his clients also facilitation (1) and (3) building capacity. The Consensus Building knowledge centre became

an institution with a business plan and consultants.
It looks rather instrumental. Differences are supposed to be barriers
that have to be removed to places where they don't harm society, like
the football field.

In contrast to Lawrence Susskind c.s., John Kolstoe and Peter Schmid
(next paragraph) chose a more practical, problem-oriented approach.
'New ideas are fuelled by differences of opinion,' Kolstoe argued. 'The
question is, where should the differences occur? In the clash of wills
and vested interests, and within the power-relationships of adversarial
systems, positions become entrenched, differences are magnified and
problems escalate. Manipulators, using power-relationships, find ways to
beat the systems and emasculate them.
'Consultation changes this. It starts with unity of purpose. Different
views are essential, but they are expressed before positions become
entrenched. The clash is not among the individuals not even among the
proposed solutions. The clash of differing opinions provides the spark
of new ideas, from which the wisdom, the energy, the concern, the
security, yes, the genius of the group, produce solutions. And that is
revolutionary.'

Method Holistic Participation
The basic principles of teamwork in construction were formulated and
successfully implemented in the 1940s by the architects Walter Gropius
and Konrad Wachsmann. They experienced the process of building as a
chain, based on cooperation. In the end it is the kind of cooperation,
together with some other factors, that decides whether a building has
quality or not. Designers, planners, financiers, administrators, managers,
builders, works foremen, suppliers, business and government, all kinds
of building-linked people and organizations are involved in the planning
- design - execution - routine of building. During this process problems
rise with respect to fine-tuning, coordination and confrontation of
interests.

Peter Schmid combined the insights of Gropius and Wachsmann with
kindred-spirited team-processes that, as he had found out, already
occurred in ancient clans and cultures. All these processes included the
approach of an issue from different angles. Schmid's method was
designed to develop solutions and to decide on other issues than

construction planning as well. Ecological and participation problems that need to be solved are incorporated in what is called Schmid's Method Holistic Participation (MHP).[203] The MHP is based on systematic teamwork and consensus building. The involved get input from experts to enhance knowledge and improve the decisions. The MHP is down to earth and constructive. It has been applied multiple times by e.g. the Dutch province of Noord-Brabant on complex societal and environmental issues that were of concern to a local community.

In one or more sessions the participants of an MHP atelier choose themes that they refer to as important and relevant. After this first step the group splits up in separated sub-groups. The number of topics has to match the number of sub-groups. After exchanging information and maybe a short conversation, the themes plus input are passed on to the next group and so on until each sub-group has covered all themes. Individual participants get informed about all themes and have the opportunity to influence the progress of the process. During the structuring of problems and issues, and the search of possible solutions the so-called topic questions can be helpful: WHO, WHAT, WHERE, WHEN, HOW & WHY.
By asking questions parties learn to understand the interests and points of view of other participants. Brainstorming is an important instrument here.

Direct democracy

One vested power player, who understood extremely well the rise and importance of the self-producing individual was President Obama of the US. When he moved into the White House something extraordinary happened. Obama, who started presidency without majority in Congress, used public opinion with remarkable virtue, reinstalling direct democracy at the same time. The White House developed an application that could be installed on telephones and the official White House information as well as the President's agenda and speeches could be followed. But there was more to it. In September 2011 the White House launched a new online app: We the People. This tool was meant to provide for simple and public participation through petitions directed at

---

[203] Prof. Emeritus TU/e Mag. Arch. Eng. Dr.h.c. Peter Schmid, ResearchEducationDesign in ScienceArtTechnologyfor PeacefulSustainableDevelopment.

the US government. 'If a petition gathers 25,000 signatures, policy officials review it and provide an official response. If Americans harness the "Power of We," the White House will respond,' thus was written on the website. And, according to the presidential staff, it worked: 'In just one short year, the White House has received more than three million signatures from the public on over fifty thousand petitions.

'Throughout American history, the right to petition government has always been an integral part in our ability to interact with and change government. Today, the right to petition continues to illustrate "the Power of We" and shows how the collective public can influence change in our government. We the People empowers the American people to participate in the traditional petition process our Founding Fathers sought to protect through a 21st century medium.
'We take petitions seriously. Petitions posted on We the People have a real impact on policy-making. The popularity of two petitions concerning online piracy (a.k.a. SOPA & PIPA) crystallized the Administration's position on the issue, which was first detailed in a response on We the People.'[204]

The president of the US himself called upon people to use their right to petition in an active way. And it appeared to be effective, as stated on the same White House website: #dontdoublemyrate

'Interest rates on Federal subsidized Stafford loans were set to go up on July 1st, 2012, a change that would have saddled more than 7 million students with an average of $1,000 each in additional debt President Obama challenged students to speak up and take to their campuses and the internet saying "Don't Double my Rate:"

'But I'm asking everyone else who's watching or following online - call your member of Congress. Email them. Write on their Facebook page. Tweet them - we've got a hashtag. Here's the hashtag for you to tweet them: #dontdoublemyrate. All right? I'm going to repeat that - the hashtag is #dontdoublemyrate. Your voice matters. Stand up. Be heard. Be counted. Tell them now is not the time to double the interest rate on your student loans.'

---

[204] Blog Action day Power We the People

Thousands of students accepted Obama's challenge, calling on elected officials and taking to Facebook and Twitter with the hashtag #DontDoubleMyRate, and they made their message heard and Congress acted, passing a bill to stop rates from going up.

As Cleisthenes installed the Council of Five Hundred in Athens and the Agora was a place where people could directly influence the conduct of their society[205], Barack Obama tried to do the same, using contemporary communication techniques. Government for the people, by the people, needs active citizenship as well as reasonable citizens. Both evoke each other, when bestowed with responsibility most people take their task seriously and learn by doing, because, like Adam Smith already stated, there are two sides to humanity: the self-centred and the moral, altruist part.

Many times these aspects of the human psychology are intertwined, since giving more than often leads to personal gain. When you give something to somebody, s/he feels obliged to give something back. This means that giving isn't losing and many times turns into winning. This principle is one of the basics on which all human societies are built. Reciprocation therefore is one of the major influencing weapons Robert Cialdini[206] described, moving on with the thinking frame Morton Deutsch explored. All human civilizations have give and take customs, traditions and regulations. These form a network of obligations. Besides that, reciprocation binds people and sets the conditions for working together. This human feature makes it possible to divide work, exchange goods and services and creates the interdependency that allows individuals to connect in efficient operating units. In other words, the characteristic reciprocation allows people to work together.

The contemporary job of government appears to be providing guidelines and stimulating a desired development, while facilitating and coaching local stakeholders. Such government requires a broader view, call it a helicopter view, of society, but does not need to interfere directly into local communities. It has to persuade people to act along for the total benefit, take care of the commons, but the individuals inside the local environments know best how to deal with their

---

[205] John Keane, Life and Death of Democracy, Edition Pocket Books, 2010
[206] Invloed, theorie en praktijk, Robert B. Cialdini, Uitgeverij Nieuwezijds, 2001

localities. Once they are persuaded of the benefits of a certain development, once they engage, act and profit in a way from the development, they organize solutions out of free will and reason. As already mentioned, the EU steers on the base of permissive consent. The rather small EC acts on large issues without consulting the Parliament for every decision. That would cause paralysis through an even larger bureaucracy. The EU parliament can call the EC to stand when member states disagree with the actions - or lack of actions - of the Committee. So can individual European citizens, through petitioning. One million signatures from seven different countries are needed. Some members of Parliament call upon citizens to let their voices be heard on certain issues through petitions, twitter, facebook. Like the Obama administration.

Direct democracy, participative democracy, consultation manners are all fashions of power to the people. They are most significant in current day developments and important tools in the theory of ecolution. Solutions can be found when traditional opponents form alliances and start to work together through consultation. Consultation is different from democracy in the way that democracy has the intrinsic of choice, meaning one will win and the other loses. Consultation gathers parties in a spirit of harmony and trust to have a dialogue on the optimal solution for a problem. Consultation is at its' best in confined circles, concerning local matters. Then all stakeholders can be equally heard and participate on equal base, build trust relationships and learn about each other's worries and interests. However, when the group gets too large, or the issue gets too big, consultation risks becoming a beer-garden.

May the best one liner win
Even if parties disagree, there still may be overall consent to move forward in order to settle the issue. For example: On October 29, 2004, the Treaty on the establishing of a Constitution for Europe was signed by representatives of the then 25 member states of the EU. Later it was ratified by 18 member states. Then the French and the Dutch referenda took place. The vote pro or against the EU Constitution was the first national referendum in the Netherlands in 200 years. A referendum conflicts with the Dutch Model of Consultation. It is a perfect tool for opportunists and populists, especially when the answer to the question is either yes or no. And although the entire text of the constitutional law

was freely available to all members of society, nearly nobody went through the trouble of fetching a copy and actually reading what this constitution was about. The Dutch government neither tried their best to explain on the European Union and why one could be in favor or against a collective constitution.

There came no greater understanding of the principles on which the EU is built. The only thing left was sentiment in a fearful society. *Angst* for foreigners, afraid of change and fear of losing whatever there was that could be lost, characterized the Dutch society at that time and these fears were fed, so easily.

In such a case a referendum has nothing to do with democracy, it has to do with demagogy. May the best one liner win. These types of referenda do not challenge voters to fill their minds with fresh knowledge and understanding. People are more likely to stick to their prejudices and animalistic fears in such a context. It is more like Russian roulette. And the bullet hit the brain. That is what happened. The Dutch ended up saying No to the EU Constitution and so did the French.

However:

Despite these popular rejections the European movement in the direction of unity and peace went on, apparently based on some kind of consent among the elected European leaders. Following a period of reflection, the Treaty of Lisbon was created to replace the Constitutional Treaty. Formulated as amendments to the existing treaties, the Treaty of Lisbon contained much if not the whole of the constitution. Signed on 13 December 2007, the Lisbon Treaty entered into force on 1 December 2009.

A city gets wise

Rotterdam is one of the Dutch cities that suffered considerable problems all at once. The issues varied from air, ground and water pollution and traffic jams to a disengaging population. These were the consequences of being Europe's main port, surrounded by heavy industry such as power plants and petrochemical clusters. Still Rotterdam needed the industry for its' economic survival. At the same time highly educated and talented people fled the city to live in a more healthy and pleasant environment, leaving the centre to those with less money and less education. Apart from this Rotterdam lays in a delta, leaving it vulnerable for rising water from the North Sea as well as from the rivers Meuse and Rhine. Starting the millennium economic, ecological and social disasters were just around the corner. But then it appeared as if the city got wise. Industry, port authority, city hall, environmental groups, university and knowledge centres, and individual citizens, decided to work together to revitalize their town and create a sustainable future together. This major operation had the objective to reduce carbon emissions to half of the amount of 1990 while doubling productivity and greening the city[207]. The alliance between the stakeholders was called the Rotterdam Climate Initiative, and what they were trying to establish was a joint effort society of some kind.

The example of Rotterdam is such a beautiful one, because this city of workers got to producing more and more sustainable innovations, such as water storage in parking lots and playgrounds and city heating through industrial residual heat, innovative financing methods that counted lifecycles, recycling waste, building energy smart and efficient. Rotterdam has also been greening the cities playgrounds together with schools, parents and children, targeting several objectives: social coherence, clean air, safe and comfortable living areas, empowering citizens and allowing kids to play outside in urban nature. Every citizen who came up with an initiative to improve the city in social, ecological and / or economic ways, can count on support of city hall, whether in obtaining licenses, finding the right partners or subsidy. A clear example of what Manfred Max-Neef called synergetic satisfaction of the fundamental human needs; subsistence, protection, affection, understanding, participation, creation, leisure, identity and freedom. It generated self-reliance and constructed traits d'union between dichotomies such as technology and nature, global processes and local activities, the personal and the social.[208]

---

[207] In 2007, the overall CO_2 emissions in Rotterdam amounted to approximately 29Mton, compared to 24Mton in 1990. Expectations are that, should no measures be taken, overall CO_2 emissions would rise to 39-46Mton by 2025. The main objective was to limit CO_2 emissions to 12Mton by 2025, 50% of the level in 1990. This meant that 27-34Mton of CO_2 emissions needed to be reduced whilst expanding the Rotterdam economy.' From the application for EU Green Capital 2014.
[208] See § Economics how it should be

Eco principles

The Natural Step[209] (TNS) incorporated the human-scale development theory of Max-Neef into designing and creating or producing principles that are general of nature, but can be applied in different situations by a variety of organizations or communities. These strategic sustainability guidelines are based on system thinking. 'Aid and encourage the forces and structures that help the system run itself,' Donella Meadows advised policymakers, politicians and entrepreneurs. 'Notice how many of those forces and structures are at the bottom of the hierarchy. Don't be an unthinking intervenor and destroy the system's own self-maintenance capacities. Before you charge in to make things better, pay attention to the value of what's already there.'[210] Keeping her consult in mind we move on with the principles of the Natural Step.

The Framework for Strategic Sustainable Development (TNS) used metaphors such as a funnel to illustrate the current industrial issues - increasing demand for materials and energy and depletion of life-supporting systems combined with decreasing natural resources and ecological and social stress. TNS plans by backcasting using four sustainability principles. After that actions have to be prioritized. These actions comply with:

1. Moving in the right direction (towards sustainability);
2. Flexible platforms that avoid dead-end investments;
3. Good business decisions (i.e. offer an adequate return on investment).

The Natural Step's understanding of what a sustainable society would look like was defined by four basic sustainability principles. These provide the description of success - the vision of a sustainable future - that we need to be able to backcast from. With the sustainability principles to guide us, we can take stock of what we're doing that is un-sustainable today, and begin to identify actions that will move us towards becoming more sustainable tomorrow.

Four basic sustainability principles by TNS[211]:

---

209 System conditions
210 Donella Meadows, Thinking in Systems, Earthscan, 2009 p. 178
211 www.thenaturalstep.org

'In a sustainable society, nature is not subject to systematically increasing...

... concentrations of substances extracted from the Earth's crust,

... concentrations of substances produced by society

... degradation by physical means, and, in that society ...

... people are not subject to conditions that systematically undermine their capacity to meet their needs.'

The Rocky Mountain Institute with frontman Amory Lovins provided an impressive amount of data, numbers and research showing business where the gain is. The book Reinventing Fire is an elaboration on Natural Capitalism, creating the next industrial revolution that was first published in 1999 by Lovins and his spouse at that time, Hunter Lovins together with Paul Hawken.

Four types of capital were identified as necessary for an economy to function properly[212]:

1. Human Capital;
2. Financial Capital;
3. Manufactured Capital;
4. Natural Capital.

'The industry uses the first three forms of capital to transform natural capital into the stuff of our daily lives.'[213] The authors asked themselves what our economy would look like if it fully valued all forms of capital, including human and natural capital and what profits this would bring to society. According to them four strategies create an economy that equally values all mentioned capitals:

1. Radical resource productivity;
2. Biomimicry;

---

[212] Natural capital includes all the familiar resources used by humans, like water, minerals, oil, trees, fish, soil and air. But it also encompasses living systems, which include grasslands, savannas, wetlands, estuaries, oceans, coral reefs, riparian corridors, tundras, and rainforests. From Natural Capitalism, creating the next industrial revolution, Lovins & Lovins, Paul Hawken, First Back Bay Paperback edition, October 2000

[213] Natural Capitalism, creating the next industrial revolution, Lovins & Lovins, Paul Hawken, First Back Bay Paperback edition, October 2000, p. 5

3. Service and flow economy;
4. Investing in natural capital.

The shared space concept

Most individuals understand from something we can call consciousness that responsibility comes with freedom. An interesting experiment in this matter has been performed in traffic regulation by traffic philosopher Hans Monderman. Instead of sidewalks, signs and traffic lights the design of the roads leaves all participants free to bike, drive or walk where and when they want. The shared space concept leaves it to the common sense and moral sentiment of the participant how to act and react in traffic.

What happened? There were less accidents and the traffic was more fluent then before when everything was regulated. In fact Monderman put the responsibility back where it belongs: with the commuter. Instead of allowing or forbidding and making the rules dominant, the car driver and the cyclist decide themselves what is the most sensible thing to do in a certain situation. Automobilists lower their speed voluntarily, look around if there are others, give way to an old lady on the bicycle et cetera. Monderman tried this approach for the first time in a very small village in Friesland, the North of the Netherlands, ending the 1970's.

Some thirty years later the Shared Space Concept was applied to Kensington Street in London as well. Ray Massey wrote in astonishment: 'Britain's longest "clutter-free" street was opened today with the aim of making cars and people co-exist harmoniously - without the need for hectoring signs and protective steel barriers. Indeed, the newly revamped Exhibition Road in the heart of London's museum quarter in Kensington, visited by millions of people from around Britain and the world, doesn't even have kerbs or pavements.'[214] 'It may sound counter-intuitive,' the article stated. This is just the type of counter-intuitive approach Forrester and Meadows spoke of, when they pondered on how to deal with systems. Hans Monderman understood how to apply the dichotomy freedom and safety to traffic.

The UK department for transport published: 'Communities Secretary,

---

[214] Britains longest clutter free street unveiled makes things safer

Eric Pickles, and Transport Secretary, Philip Hammond, are concerned that the character of the country's urban spaces is being damaged and have written to councils leaders calling on them to reduce the number of signs and other "street clutter".' Eric Pickles: 'Organisations like Civic Voice, Living Streets and Fixmystreet can help councils provide a Big Society solution - local people carrying out street audits will bring power and character back to neighbourhoods.'[215] Indeed this is an example of a joint effort societal approach that finds solutions through participation, not so much through regulation.

Selforganization in control circuits

The shared Space Concept in transport uses the selforganization capability of traffic. Selforganization is a spontaneous order. The system approach recognizes it as construction. Destruction would have led to accommodation or submissiveness. Construction has been possible because of reframing and changing paradigms. Selforganization generally refers to the paradigms that maintain or create a system, but here the concept is mainly used to describe how a system is built. We speak of selforganization when team members spontaneously cooperate, without being told to do so. The involved act out of own motives. And when things go right without interference do not touch them, Donella Meadows warned.[216]

An invitation for the gathering 'Selforganization & Coordination' the Royal Academy of Arts and Sciences sent in September 2009, defined the concept as follows: 'Selforganization is a universal process in which structures grow spontaneous inside a chaotic system. These structures can obtain new, own characteristics (emergence). In this context spontaneous means that there is nothing or no one that designs these structures on purpose. Organization, including selforganization, needs energy. The entropy of an organized system is smaller than that of an unorganized system. Selforganization is an elementary concept in biology, mathematics, physics, ecology, sociology and economy. It explains the origin of life, the effective working of the free market and the functioning of democratic states. Characteristic to selforganization is the simplicity of the basic rules of action and reaction that can produce very complex and yet stable systems.'

---

[215] UK government press-release
[216] Donella Meadows, Thinking in Systems, Earthscan, 2009, p. 178

Herman van Gunsteren, Professor Emeritus Political Theories of the Leiden University, was one of the lecturers during this meeting. Van Gunsteren defined four 'principles' of selforganization[217]:

1. Diversity is elementary to all types of selforganization. A condition for diversity is the freedom of expression, of movement, of organization and gathering and of undertaking;
2. Multiple mapping: imaginary maps that contain traces of former reactions to events, in order to know if an event is actually new;
3. Selection. Diversity is a beautiful thing, but if this diversity leads to nothing, it doesn't mean anything. Selection guides individual behaviour;
4. Indirect control. Direct control over the whole process of selforganization is impossible.

The elements in a selforganizing system are selfsteering. For individuals or groups this means 'the extend to which someone - an individual or a collective - feels bound to the desires, wishes, regulations and commands of a higher control circuit'.

There are eight control circuits to distinguish:
1. The individual
2. The group
3. The neighbourhood
4. The quarter
5. The community
6. The region/province
7. The country/state
8. The Federation or Union of States

Edward Goldsmith and his fellow editors of The Ecologist Magazine, who together with 34 biologists, economists and medici composed A Blueprint for Survival in 1972, have thought about the maximum size of control circuits. Face-to-face communities are the preferred size, since they support social responsibility of a kind that is not anonymous like large-scale industrial bodies and big cities are. Goldsmith c.s. came up

[217] Herman van Gunsteren, Vertrouwen in democratie, Over de principes van zelforganisatie, van Gennep Amsterdam, 2006

with neighbourhoods of 500 people that are represented in local communities of 5000 and embedded in regions of 500.000 inhabitants. Through such control circuits community feeling and global awareness are created instead of what Goldsmith c.s. called the dangerous and sterile compromises of nationalism.[218] Decentralization of decisionmaking leads to self-sufficient communities that will diminish the stress on eco-systems.

As long as selforganization of a control circuit has no negative impact on the larger circuit, there is little reasoning against it. The will to exercise power over another is non-valid in a culture where individualism, personal responsibility and freedom are prevalent. Aid and encourage the forces and structures that help the system run itself,' Donella Meadows advised policy makers, politicians and entrepreneurs. 'Notice how many of those forces and structures are at the bottom of the hierarchy. Don't be an unthinking intervenor and destroy the system's own self-maintenance capacities. Before you charge in to make things better, pay attention to the value of what's already there.'[219]

Principles and guidelines direct the process, project or development focus on the main aspects, while the implementation and completion happens de-central in the greatest possible freedom. Alderman Adri Duivesteijn applied such a Principle Approach in the Dutch city Almere at an urban development project.

Principles for building homes[220]
In the Dutch town Almere Alderman Duivesteijn initiated developing houses and building these according to principles, in 2008. It is an example of researching regimen on location. The seven principles are:

1. Cherish diversity;
2. Connect location to context;
3. Combine city and nature;
4. Anticipate change;
5. Keep innovating;

[218] Andrew Dobson (ed.), The Green Reader, p 73 - 76
[219] Thinking in Systems, Donella H. Meadows, Earthscan, London, 2009, p. 178
[220] Cradle to cradle website, Project Almere, January 2009

6. Design healthy systems;
7. People create the town.

Each principle is guided by a Cradle to Cradle-text of the American architect McDonough. For instance principle 6: 'Wouldn't it be wonderful if we could be proud on our industry instead of feeling guilty for it? If new buildings resembled trees and provided for shadow, for living area for singing birds, food, energy and clean water?'

Unity gives Strength

Around 1550 the motto for the area that would become the Republic of the Seven United Netherlands (1579, Union of Utrecht) was Eendracht maakt Macht. In English: Unity gives Strength. Unity can grow spontaneously, but needs to be supported and facilitated by institutions, a word with many meanings. Hayami and Ruttan (1985) came up with a definition of an institution: 'Institutions are the rules of a society or of organizations that facilitate coordination among people by helping them form expectations, which each person can reasonably hold in dealing with others.'[221]

There are many ways that lead from Me to We[222]. Almost always they run through one or more institutions. If those institutions are deconstructed from time to time, it will work out fine. If expectations are adapted to the new situation, people change their behaviour, technology and decisions according to such a change in expectations. That is why.

There is no World Government that can make laws and rules for almost 200 nation states and more than seven billion people on Earth and there is no World Police to maintain order if things get out of control. And if we had such institutions it wouldn't work. As a consequence no man's land stretches beyond the nation state, or in economical terms: the commons. Here the right of the strongest rules. Small countries like the Netherlands, Belgium and Denmark don't make it on global level. They are determined to play the second or third violin, unless they join forces.

---

[221] Can Economic Growth Be Sustained? The Collected Papers of Vernon W. Ruttan and Yujiro Hayami, ed. By Keijiro Otsuka and C. Ford Runge, Oxford University Press, 2011, p. 302
[222] See § The art of consultation

That is what 27 European countries did. Of those 27 EU-members 17 have introduced the euro and thereby gave up monetary instruments like interest policies that may be used to support the national economy. A loss of autonomy apparently is valued lower than a gain in economical power and consequently in wealth by joining forces. There is a reason for introducing and containing the euro. The sum of 17 small, open economies together forms one large closed economy. In this particular closed economy, that is called 'Euroland' on average two-third of every euro spent goes to one of the 17 member-countries, strengthening the economy of Euroland as a whole. It is a matter of 'united we stand, united we fall'.

A closed economy has completely different characteristics than an open economy from a macro-economic point of view. If, for example the wages and all other incomes rise with say € 900 per person, about € 600 pp bolsters the economy of Euroland. If there is room (capacity) for a higher production of goods and services, the result will be: more jobs, steady prices and more business revenues.

On the other hand, if in a small, open economy € 800 of the extra income per capita is spent on electronics from abroad, imports rise in relation to exports, which may lead to a deficit on the current account and as a consequence the national currency will weaken. Results: higher interest, inflation and unemployment. Policy makers in a closed economy don't have to worry so much about that.

The main point here is, that the founders of the EU have created strong institutions that are overarching several nation states and take over more and more tasks and instruments from these nation states. By the way, the whole idea is about establishing peace: Unity in diversity.

Institutionalization of Human Rights

It is no accident that history gave birth to two peace institutes around the same time, just after WWII. Next to the forerunner of the EU, the ECSC, the United Nations was founded in 1945. The initiative gathered 51 states then and now has grown into an organization of 193 countries, of which South Sudan became the youngest sprout in 2011. The Universal Declaration of Human Rights[223] is the main and foremost

---

[223] The Declaration of Universal Human Rights dates from 1948. It explicitly defends the freedom and rights of each individual. It can provide guidelines for actions, so can the Millennium Goals or Earth Charter.

ambitious document issued by the organization that welcomes visitors to its website with the words: 'Welcome to the United Nations. It's your world.' The first article of the Declaration of Human Rights reads as follows: 'All human beings are born free and equal in dignity and rights. They are endowed with reason and conscience and should act towards one another in a spirit of brotherhood.'[224]

The first article uses brotherhood (fraternity) to overarch the dichotomy freedom and equality, like the French revolution did - Liberté, Egalité & Fraternité. It combines rights with responsibility and reason and obliges to act, which reminds of the French philosopher Jean Paul Sartre who stated: 'There is no other reality then action. Man is his/her own design. She/He exists to the extent to which she/he realizes her/himself. Man is nothing more then the sum of his/her deeds, nothing different from his/her own life.[225]

Limited power and legitimate claims

The Declaration of Universal Human Rights however has been under severe scrutiny ever since the ink on the paper it was written on dried. Amartya Sen enumerated three critiques in his book Development as Freedom[226]:

1. The legitimacy critique
2. The coherence critique
3. The cultural critique

In short the first, legitimacy critique, can be explained as 'an insistence that rights must be seen in postinstitutional terms as instruments, rather than as a prior ethical entitlement'. Sen argued that this type of critique misses the point of the exercise. The Declaration of Universal Human Rights should be seen as 'a demand, which is justified by the ethical importance of acknowledging that certain rights are appropriate entitlements of all human beings'.

The second critique involves the duty to enforce the human rights. If

---

[224] Universal Declaration of Human Rights, article 1
[225] Jean Paul Sartre, Over het existentialisme, AW Bruna & Zoon, Utrecht/Aartselaar, p.33/34
[226] Amartya Sen, Development as Freedom, Oxford Press, 1999, p 227 - 232

one person enjoys rights there has to be another person that provides these. Whose duty is it to enforce the human rights? According to Amartya Sen 'Human rights are seen as rights shared by all - irrespective citizenship - the benefits of which everyone should have. [....] [Therefore] the claims can be generally addressed to all those who are in a position to help'.

JES! would like to add that international courts, such as the International Criminal Court (ICC) in The Hague and the European Court for Human Rights increasingly both are able to solve the legitimacy as well as the coherence critiques.

The ICC was founded after broad international consent rose on the necessity to end impunity for perpetrators of the most serious crimes, such as genocide. This was after the International Criminal Tribunals for the former Yugoslavia and for Rwanda took place. The ICC started to operate at the same time Mr. Sen's book Development as Freedom was published, in 1999.

Although countries such as the USA and Israel failed to acknowledge the court and despite the argument that not all injured human rights can be brought to justice at The Hague it is a broadly carried international (121 countries) legal institution, governed by the Rome Statute, which enforces human rights.

Former warlord and dictator Charles Taylor of Liberia stood trial at the ICC for crimes against humanity and was sentenced to fifty years in prison on May 30, 2012. The Libyan Transitional Government was pressured to extradite the son of Muammar Gaddafi, Saif Al-Islam Gaddafi, to be tried for murder and persecution. These two examples can be perceived as serious warnings issued by the international community to those that commit hideous crimes. No impunity any more, not even for the leaders of nations.

International cooperation and legislation that protects citizens against even their own governments and punishes those found guilty of cruel crimes is a big step in the rights direction for humanity. Apart from the protection, recognition and possible claims the victims of these criminals obtain, it is also a characteristic of civilization to try suspects in a court, enable them to defend themselves against allegations and punish according to the law. The ICC is about justice for all. This is a much more peaceful and sophisticated solution then allowing angry mobs to demolish the suspect, like happened to Gaddafi senior when the Libyan freedom fighters found him in his hideout. From hate nothing can come but hate. In that aspect it surely is regrettable that Libyan rebels took their own revenge.

The other international cooperation on the rights of civilians of multiple nations is the European Court for Human Rights (ECHR). The ECHR has a different objective than the International Criminal Court. It is founded in 1959 to scrutinize European governments with respect to civil and political rights as have been set out in the European Convention on Human Rights. Individuals can apply to the ECHR directly. Although in the brochure 'The court in brief' the ECHR stated that it is not to be confused with the Declaration of Universal Human Rights, there are certainly important overlaps in vision, such as the emphases on freedom of expression. The European Convention on Human Rights dates from the same era as the Declaration of Universal Human Rights. It was written in 1950 and entered into force in 1953.

The European Convention on Human Rights secures in particular:
* The right to life,
* The right to a fair hearing,
* The right to respect for private and family life,
* Freedom of expression,
* Freedom of thought, conscience and religion,
* The protection of property.

The Convention prohibits in particular:
* Torture and inhuman or degrading treatment or punishment,
* Slavery and forced labour,
* Death penalty,
* Arbitrary and unlawful detention,
* Discrimination in the enjoyment of the rights and freedoms set out in the Convention.[227]

The decision to expand the solutionfinding cluster technology of the ecolution matrix with institutionalization came forth out the importance

---

[227] From the Court in Brief, ECHR pdf

of institutes such as the ICC and ECHR. Institutes can enforce change, were individuals lack the resources. And although, speaking from experience, the ECHR - and ICC as well - paces the tempo of an old man, an application can take five to six years before it is taken into consideration, and justice is not always done, institutionalized international law enforcement to protect basic civil and political rights is a virtue of the current society. At the same time institutes can obstruct developments in a society, when they grow slack, when the rules become dominant over the people. 'A productive institute bends the rules towards the individual,' a former major of Uden, a small town in Brabant said some years ago.

Cultural paradigms

The third critique on the Declaration of Universal Human Rights may be the most common and hardest to oppose since it is arouses fierce emotions. Cultural values differ from community to community and they carry deeply rooted paradigms. The emphases that Western society for example puts on individual freedoms is a thorn in the flesh of many Muslim leaders and quite often of the communities led by them. As we have seen even in a freedom loving country as the Netherlands there are parties who (want to) deny women political influence, which is a profound unfreedom.

In Islam communities it is considered blasphemy - one of the worst crimes thinkable - to draw a picture of the Prophet Mohammed or to utter the slightest critique on the Qur'an. Some tend to take the Holy Script literally and apply regulations, such as strict interpretations of the Sharia that were written down in the year 600, to contemporary society. Just like the Dutch Political Reformational Party tends to do with the Bible. The West considers this religious conservatism an extreme threat to freedom of expression and freedom of religion, not in the least because Church (Mosque) and State are inseparable according to the same interpretation of Islam. Many crimes against humanity have been committed in the name of God by all main religions. A narrow interpretation of (religious) prescriptions evokes power abuse and allows the greedy to fill their already full baskets. Especially when the followers are uneducated, authority conscious (obedient) and fall into the trap of eloquent rhetoric and fear sowing words.

Throughout history the blasphemy accusation has brought a lot of misery for many individuals and whole societies. In Europe the Spanish Inquisition is such example of utmost wrongdoing.

More recently massive abuse of young boys by priests of the Catholic Church has come out. It took half a lifetime for the abused to speak up. Should a blasphemy law still have been a powerful instrument in these areas, this black page of the Catholic Church would have remained in the dark, leaving the victims out on their own.

Blasphemy is an easy accusation. Especially when it concerns religious minorities, dissidents or weaker members of a society. In Russia three members of a punk group called Pussy Riot were convicted to imprisonment on August 17, 2012. The verdict was blasphemy, but the real 'crime' the girls committed was criticizing Vladimir Putin's rule. Pakistan too provided proof for the destructivity of this type of legislation.

Pakistan's Black Law[228]

Asia Bibi is on death row in a Pakistan jail. She has been imprisoned on June 14, 2009. The crime she committed: blasphemy. The French Anne Isabelle Tollet wrote her story. The book is called Blasphème. Mrs Tollet used Asia's own words and recordings. Asia is in a prison cell in which she can touch both walls just by spreading her arms. There are no sanitary provisions, no windows. And it is hot. Mrs Tollet was not allowed to visit Asia. She interviewed her through her husband who can visit once a week.

The family is on the run, from shelter to shelter, but they have a small income: the revenues of the book. Ironically Asia's own daughters will not be able to read it. They don't go to school due to the continuous running and hiding.

The story goes something like this. Asia, an illiterate Christian mother of five, worked in the fields with other women from the village where she lived. The other women, without exception, worshipped Allah. The work was hard that day. It was warm, 45° Celsius in the shade. Asia got thirsty. She went to the well to drink a little water. Her colleagues accused her of impuring the water with her Christian thirst. Asia replied to her co-workers that in her view the prophet Mohammed

---

[228] Based on articles from nonfiXe blogspot: Pakistan's Black Law, Rimsha en de godslasteraars, and Rimsha en de dollars

would not mind them drinking from the same cup. This was a mistake. But she could make up for it. The only thing she had to do was to convert to Islam. 'I respect Islam and the Prophet Mohammed', Asia allegedly replied, but I believe in Jesus Christ'. These answers signed her death verdict. The women went to the local Mullah and he arranged for Asia to be arrested and thrown in jail. It has been more than three years today, September 2012.

In Pakistan the Blasphemy Law is the most feared and oppressive legal rule. It is commonly known (and a much used tool) that the accusation of blasphemy alone is enough to ruin an opponents' life. In theory the law, also known as Black Law, protects all religions equally, Islam as much as Christianity, Judaism or Hinduism. But in this country with a 97% Muslim population, minorities live the harsh life. Christians try to go by unnoticed. They work the lower jobs and live in poor conditions. Of all convicted under the Black Law 50% is Muslim, the other half is of a different religion. Three percent of the population delivers half of the convicted blasphemers.

Asia Bibi is one of them and the only woman on death row. She was supported by the Muslim governor of her region Punjab, Mr. Salman Taseer, and by the Minister of Minorities, Mr. Shahbaz Bhatti. Both leaders have been brutally killed because of their public support for Asia and for questioning the Blasphemy law.
Islamic fundamentalists threaten to throw the country into chaos, should the government try to change this draconic version of both the Sharia Law and its' previous European sibling implemented by the Spanish Inquisition. Most common Pakistani seem to endure this sword of Damocles submissively.

In August 2012 a young Christian girl named Rimsha Masih was arrested for burning pages of the Qur'an. Charges: Blasphemy. The girl was no older then fourteen years. She was as innocent as a flower in springtime, due to her young age and allegedly suffering of Down's syndrome. Illiterate and poor Rimsha lived in a run-down shack in one of Islamabad's slums. Her arrest led to worldwide protests. Especially when it came out that three witnesses had seen how the local Mullah tore some pages out of a Qur'an and placed them with the ashes that were the proof of Rimsha's blasphemy.

Young Rimsha stayed in a heavily guarded prison for more then three weeks before the judge granted her bail. This was the same prison where the murderer of Governor Taseer is being held. That man, by the way, is widely praised for his crime: 'killing a blasphemer'.

In Rimsha's story a rejected lover, a greedy landowner and powerplay by a little Mullah added up to the events that made the girl victim to the Black Law. She was an easy target, at least so it seemed. Her allegedly blasphemous act led to the Christians fleeing the neighbourhood, making room for more worshippers in the local Mosque. The international row as well as protesting Pakistani civilians saved Rimsha from rotting in a cell for many years.

Moreover, Rimsha has become the first person able to bail out under the Black Law. That is the good news, setting a precedent for other courts. But, the bail was 1 million Pakistani rupees ($ 10.500) an enormous amount of money for a girl from the slums. An awkward decision too, the bail sum was twice the price that fundamentalists put on the head of Asia. Extremists apparently are afraid the Pakistani authorities will not execute the death verdict. The local Mullah Qari Mohammed Salim reacted to BBC News: 'If the law punishes somebody for blasphemy, and that person is pardoned, then we will take the law in our hands'.

As unlikely as it is for Asia to regain her freedom, it is for Rimsha. Even after her bail is set and she is out of prison. Apart from the police investigation that goes on, and can flip like a coin from one side to the other, she risks being violated, even killed, by a vigilante group or a silent aggressor, like other accused blasphemers have been before.

On the day of her release on bail, an armoured vehicle packed with guards drove her to a military helicopter. She was reunited with her family in a secret place.

One young girl, one forty-four year old mother and many others suffer under the Black Law that has Pakistan in its' grip. Politicians are afraid to tackle it. Judges and lawyers flee the country after defending its' victims.

Pakistan seems to be in deadlock, but at least there is some movement and discussion over the Black Law. Muslim leaders are open for a change, a small change, but a change: Accusers of blasphemy that come

up with false allegations will be judged under the same law. This is what has happened to the Mullah who allegedly framed Rimsha.
This minor change may lead to less false accusations after personal disputes and vendetta's and at least some sort of dialogue on the Black Law started, but it is no way near a real solution for the Pakistani civil society.

Dimensions of power

A much-used argument in the defense of draconic rules such as the Pakistani black law is that of cultural values and religious identity. The falseness of this reasoning is that a) apparently the values and identity of one group are more important than those of the other, weaker or smaller group. b) This type of legislation puts uncontrollable power in the hands of some. c) Such rules destruct the creativity and solutionfinding abilities of a society. Blasphemy laws obstruct all forms of sustainable development and are in contrast with fundamental human freedoms and rights.

We can determine four types of power[229]. Destructive regulations lead to the first, the power over somebody else.

1. Power over: The ability to dominate. This form of power is finite, so that if someone obtains more power then it automatically leads to someone else having less power;
2. Power to: The ability to see possibilities for change;
3. Power with: The power that comes from individuals working together collectively to achieve common goals;
4. Power within: Feelings of self-worth and self-esteem that come from within individuals.

The power over (1) a person is limited to that person's belief and conviction (paradigms) on the legitimacy and unavoidability of a certain existing hierarchy. Especially bonded people appear vulnerable to the idea they are in a way inferior, not entitled, or in debt to their abusers. Accommodation to poverty, because it makes no sense to 'try to become a quarter, when born to be a dime'[230], starts to diminish when a

---

[229] Just Associates, Lisa Veneklasen and Valerie Miller, A New Weave, The Action Guide for Advocacy and Citizen Participation, p. 45
[230] The old Dutch proverb 'Als je voor een dubbeltje geboren bent, kun je nooit

person obtains the power to (2) act for herself and obtains results, sees change, comes to understand the limits of the power held over her. Such can also be obtained when people act together (3) and find they can do, as the Tunisian student Emna found out during the Arab revolution of 2010/11. 'We [Tunisians] will not accept dictatorship anymore. We have lived it and now we have toppled it. We know now we can make a change. I am sure my country will enter democracy, just because it is the people's will.'[231]

The next level is to find the power within (4). Individuals who have such power will not succumb to circumstances or limitations to live the life they have reason to value put upon them by exterior parties. The latter is real empowerment and a concept that can take individuals and the communities or organizations they are part of towards a higher level of living together.

The Right to Development

Whereas countries, companies and individuals have self-centred motives, at least partial, to support others in the attempt for a better life, when they unite and form institutes on shared visions the support becomes more objective, like the enforcement of the Declaration of the Universal Human Rights. In 1986 the Right to Development was added to the original document.

'I am duty-bound to raise this anniversary call. We must end discrimination in the distribution of the benefits of development. We must stop the 500,000 preventable deaths of women in childbirth every year. We must free the millions of children from hunger in a world of plenty. And we must ensure that people can benefit from their country's natural resources and participate meaningfully in decision-making. These are the kind of issues addressed by the Declaration, which calls for equal opportunity and a just social order. ... It's not an act of nature that leaves more than one billion people around the world locked in the jaws of poverty. It's a result of the denial of their fundamental human

---

een kwartje worden' expresses a disbelief in social mobility. A person will not be able to rise from the class where he or she is born in.

[231] This remark was made by Emna when discussing the 'threat of Muslim dominance and implementation of Sharia law' in her country Tunisia where the Islamic Ennaddha party won a majority in the constituent assembly, October 2011.

right to development.'[232]
This passionate plea was expressed by High Commissioner for Human Rights, Mrs. Navi Pillay, on the 25th anniversary of the Declaration of the Right to Development, which became an inalienable human right in 1986.[233]

Navi Pillay, a former lawyer from South Africa, experienced deprivation first hand. Being the daughter of a bus driver of Indian origin Apartheid inflicted as much injustice on her as it did on all other non-white citizens in the country. Navi Pillay (1941) reportedly was able to study at the University of Natal because the local Indian Community supported her with donations. Later she became the first South African who obtained a degree from Harvard Law School. However, no firm would employ her, since it was inconceivable for white persons to get orders from a colored person. Navi Pillay started her own law practice. She defended anti-apartheid activists, protested against torture and fought the poor circumstances of political prisoners. She was her own husband's lawyer when he got convicted under Apartheid Laws. In 1973 she successfully defended the right to have access to a lawyer for the prisoners on Robben Island, where also Nelson Mandela was detained. She advocated women's rights, and ran a shelter for victims of domestic violence and co-founded several women's rights groups among which Equality Now. During her 28 years long work in South Africa, she never was allowed in the judge room, because of the color of her skin. However in 1995, when Apartheid was abolished Nelson Mandela nominated Navi Pillay the first colored woman to the High Court of South Africa.

She held this position only for a short time. In the same year she was appointed judge on the International Criminal Tribunal for Rwanda, where she served a total of eight years, the last four (1999-2003) as President. The Rwanda Tribunal was the first international court to convict genocide and set a landmark for women rights by declaring rape a crime of war.

Navi Pillay: 'The Right to Development can be realized only when there

[232] Navi Pillay, High Commissioner of Human Rights at the 25th anniversary of the Right to Development. From the website of the UN, 2011.
[233] The Declaration of the Right to Development

is a solid national and international accountability framework for development that respects social justice and human rights. Let us return to the hopeful and principled message of the Declaration itself - in a spirit of reasoned compromise and with a sense of the vital mission at hand, and focus our efforts on making the right to development a reality for all.'

The Right to Development has been defined as an inalienable right, declaring that everyone is 'entitled to participate in, contribute to, and enjoy economic, social, cultural and political development, in which all human rights and fundamental freedoms can be fully realized'.[234]

Despite all efforts and promising words the same UN reported on an increasing amount of people suffering from malnourishment - 850 million people were hungry in 1980. In the 2010's the number has grown to 1 billion underfed men, women and children. 'Despite over thirty years of technological progress and ever-increasing exploitation of natural resources, 150 million more people are now malnourished. 'Rampant poverty and stark inequalities, both within and across countries, serve as a constant reminder that the 1948 Universal Declaration of Human Rights, the fundamental principles of international human rights law it subsequently inspired, and indeed the 1986 Declaration on the Right to Development remain empty words for far too many people, especially those belonging to marginalized groups.'[235]

Sustainable Development Solutions Network
August 2012, High Commissioner of the United Nations, Mr. Ban Ki Moon announced the formation of the Sustainable Development Solutions Network (SDSN) using the following introduction: 'The scale of the global sustainable development challenge is unprecedented. The fight against extreme poverty has made great progress under the Millennium Development Goals (MDGs), but more than 1 billion people continue to live in extreme poverty. Inequality and social exclusion are widening within most countries. As the world population is estimated to rise to 9 billion by 2050 and global GDP to more than US$200 trillion, the world urgently needs to address the sustainable

---

[234] See Development is a Human Right
[235] See Right to Development, Background

development challenges of ending poverty, increasing social inclusion, and sustaining the planet.' As a matter of fact the UN started a global web of Ecolution Centres[236] inviting scientists, civil society and the private sector to join forces and search for solutions at local, national and international level. The SDSN aims at triple loop learning and cumulative learning in search of a holistic approach: 'This Network will accelerate joint learning and help to overcome the compartmentalization of technical and policy work by promoting integrated approaches to the interconnected economic, social, and environmental challenges confronting the world'.[237]

Conscious capitalism

Technological inventions have been the smoothening change throughout history. They are easy to agree on, do not require behaviour change, at least not at the time of introduction. New techniques are perceived sexy by most manufacturers and engineers and re-establish man's intellectual dominance over nature. Yet the time has come for behaviour change, next to technological solutions. For God & the Engineers cannot solve greed, obesity and large communities getting screwed over and over again. In the age of the End of Competition, set in by depletion of life-supporting resources, Self Interest and reciprocity will push towards cooperation and sharing. Business is already starting to socialize and co-create, co-design, co-develop, out of the realization that business is co-dependent of the rest of society. This attitude, that comes down to behaviour (combined with innovation, sound institutionalization and democratic decisionmaking forms), is profitable in many a way in the age of the End of Competition.

Ron Shaich, founder, Chairman and Co-CEO of Panera Bread, a 1600 bakery café chain in the US, posted an article on Linkedin on October 9, 2012, that began with the following words: 'I recently heard that the only group held in lower regard than corporate executives in the United

---

[236] Bakker & Van Empel recommended the foundation of regional Ecolution Centres in order to explore and experiment with behaviour change, technologies and ways of decision making, to develop and disseminate knowledge and skills and up- scale successful projects. In these centres businesses, governments, scientists, scholars cooperate to create mutual gains solutions, which are shared with other Ecolution Centres or interested parties. Allemaal Winnen, Studio nonfiXe, 2012
[237] See the website Sustainable Development Solutions Network, Vision and Organization

States is Congress. Wow! Think about that. What a terrible blow to business. And yet, I'd argue it's our own fault. By serving narrow self-interests, we - the nation's business leaders - earned the country's mistrust. We have been purveyors of our own doom.'

Mr. Shaich sensed things had taken the wrong turn, and when people walk away from business, business is over. The business community, he felt, is responsible for restoring its' own lustre. He understood that changing the patterns and actions of his company is in the interest of the firm, as well as beneficial for his self-esteem. Ron Shaich rejected the 'narrow self-interests' and shortsightedness in doing business. He also came to grips with the responsibility that broad, free shoulders have to bear, in order to maintain the freedom and the well-developed, well-fed body.

Panera Bread thought of its' own socialization and talents. One of the competencies was organizational capacity that is so typical for large enterprises and often lacked by charity or NGO's. Ron Shaich wrote: 'Our belief was that our operation's national scale provided Panera with an opportunity to turn that core competency against a societal ill and uniquely make a difference in addressing the food insecurity in this country. We continued to kick the tires on this idea and decided: we were going to tackle an issue using our skills and sweat equity rather than, say, hand-outs or day-end product donations, which Panera had been doing, and continued to do, through its Dough Nation program.' Some years ago Panera opened the first Panera Care Café that was the same as every other settlement of the company but for one, important, characteristic. At the Care Café there was no cash register. Instead a donation box had been placed. Customers paid what they valued the product, voluntarily. Those who had no money, did not pay, but could eat and were honoured like paying clients.

In 2012 Panera had opened four Care Café's. According to the companies CEO these bars were sustainable. 'Food banks serve a vital function, but they are often disorganized and inefficient,' Ron Shaich pondered and moved on with a call to other businessmen and women, challenging them to think different and act social, or as he called it: conscious capitalism. 'Rethinking why our respective organizations exist might change the public's perception that capitalism is wrong or even "evil." Businesses won't be stigmatized for making money if they are truly conscious about their place and purpose in society. More importantly, contributing what we do best will make a difference in our communities.'[238] The Panera Bread Café CEO put to work three of Robert Cialdini's weapons of influence: the reciprocal principle, consistency (combined with commitment) and the social proof concept. The first, give and take, is the most powerful according to Cialdini[239]. It allows societies to evolve, for it means that giving something does not mean losing. When a person gives something to somebody else, the other person will feel obliged to give something back, or grant a wish. This implicates that when Mr. Shaich offers coffee, most are inclined to put some money in the donation box. Maybe even more than the price of the coffee would have been in a regular Bread Café.

It has to do with consistency as well. People like the concept of large organizations making an effort to feed the hungry. People also like the freedom of choice to pay or not (although this freedom is limited, due to all three factors of influence discussed here) and to decide for themselves how to value the food and beverages. Talking about the initiative with enthusiasm to friends, or writing about it, evokes the natural desire to act in line with previous words (and deeds). People will be more inclined to put a donation in the box. Humans act according to their self-image.

The third principle of influence is social proof. It means something like, looking at others (preferably peers) to find out how to react upon a situation. Between the other guests in one of Ron Shaich's café's most people don't want to stand out as a freerider, a sponger, so they will pay for their food and beverages. These three human features might very well reward the Panera socialization of its' business more than the gains would have been while doing business as usual.

The ethics of business
Ron Shaich is the unlisted member of a growing group of individuals that decided to go for change. These people leave the profit only paradigm and start to socialize business out of understanding there is a mutual dependency and interference of profit, planet and people. With

---

[238] Corporations must become Socially Conscious Citizens, Ron Shaich, LinkedIn, Oct 9, 2012
[239] Invloed, theorie en praktijk, Robert B. Cialdini, Uitgeverij Nieuwezijds, 2001

these kinds of individuals, all of them unlisted, organizations come along. For Shaich has 1600 bakery café's in his backpack. Bill and Melinda Gates, for example, have even more cloud, financially as well as organizational. So do Kofi Annan, Jeffrey Skoll and Bill Clinton. Or actor Leonardo Di Capri, who wanted to save the Antarctic Ocean, Pop idols like Bono, Madonna, Bob Geldoff et cetera. The socialized businesses are able to do something charity apparently is incapable of: organizing. Businesses are organizational experts. They know how to produce as efficient and effective as possible, understand logistics, marketing and are solutionfinding organisms by nature, for survival. The ethics of business in the West used to be profit driven. Long term relationships, trust, efficient use of materials, taking care of employees and satisfying clients were all underlying activities and mentalities to enlarge the profit. But profit came first. Human capital[240] - education, training, health care and social security - only counted as far as it improved the productivity of the workforce. The goal of business in the 1970's and 1980's was just that: maximizing profit for the shareholders. Milton Friedman gave a clear description related to an enterprise's social responsibility: 'the only one responsibility of business towards society is the maximization of profits to the shareholders within the legal framework and the ethical custom of the country'.[241]

Now some business is starting to understand that a profit-drive benefitting shareholders alone is not enough to motivate the personal, to keep the customers et cetera. In order to stay in business other, real intrinsic - sustainable - goals need to be aimed at as well: investments in social and natural capital come into sight.

Creating shared value

Michael Porter and Mark Kramer wrote in the Harvard Business Review about the interdependence of businesses and the societies they operate

---

[240] Natural Resource Endowment: A Mixed Blessing? Thorvaldur Gylfason, University of Iceland, drawn from the lecture at the seminar on Natural Resources, finance, and development, Algiers, November 2012. Prof. Gylfason determines 6 capitals, among which human capital, as described in the text and social capital: 'Democracy, freedom, and honesty - that is absence of corruption - to build up social capital, to strengthen the social fabric, the glue that helps hold the economic system together and keep it in good running order'.

[241] The social responsibility of business is to increase its profits. Friedman, M. The New York Times Magazine, 1970, September 13, p. 2

in. They proposed a business strategy of creating shared value - based on well understood self-interest: 'The concept of shared value, in contrast, recognizes that societal needs, not just conventional economic needs, define markets. It also recognizes that social harms and weaknesses frequently create internal costs for firms - such as wasted energy or raw materials, costly accidents and the need for remedial training to compensate for inadequacies in education. And addressing societal harms and constraints does not necessarily raise costs for firms, because they can innovate through using new technologies, operating methods, and management approaches - and as a result, increase their productivity and expand their markets. Shared value, then, is not about personal values. Nor is it about "sharing" the value already created by firms - a redistribution approach. Instead, it is about expanding the total pool of economic and social value.[242]

Further on in the same text: 'Companies can create economic value by creating societal value. There are three distinct ways to do this: by reconceiving products and markets, redefining productivity in the value chain, and building supportive industry clusters at the company's locations. Each of these is part of the virtuous circle of shared value; improving value in one area gives rise to opportunities in the others. The concept of shared value resets the boundaries of capitalism. By better connecting companies' success with societal improvement, it opens up many ways to serve new needs, gain efficiency, create differentiation, and expand markets.'[243]

The concept of shared value benefits business as well as society. In an earlier publication Porter and Kramer suggested cooperation between firms for larger issues, such as corruption in a country where they operate. 'The principle of sustainability appeals to enlightened self-interest, often invoking the so-called triple bottom line of economic, social, and environmental performance. In other words, companies should operate in ways that secure long-term economic performance by avoiding short-term behaviour that is socially detrimental or environmentally wasteful. [...] The essential test that should guide CSR is not whether a cause is worthy but whether it presents an opportunity to create shared value - that is, a meaningful benefit for society that is

---

[242] Porter & Kramer, Creating Shared Value, Harvard Business Revue, Jan. 2011
[243] Porter & Kramer, Creating Shared Value, Harvard Business Revue, Jan. 2011

also valuable to the business. Where a social issue is salient for many companies across multiple industries, it can often be addressed most effectively through cooperative models. The Extractive Industries Transparency Initiative, for example, includes 19 major oil, gas, and mining companies that have agreed to discourage corruption through full public disclosure and verification of all corporate payments to governments in the countries in which they operate. Collective action by all major corporations in these industries prevents corrupt governments from undermining social benefit by simply choosing not to deal with the firms that disclose their payments.'[244]

The socializing multinationals and their (former) CEO's are accompanied by smaller, but no less persevere persons, such as the neighbours – both running very successive businesses - who support Kenyan women contaminated with HIV, trying to empower them through information on health, education and micro financing. Or the friends - working as independent professionals - who have a foundation that operates in Gambia, teaching skills to young people and building hospitals. The number of individual well-doers seems to be rising by the day. They use their capabilities, business experience and organizational capacity to address societal needs. On the other hand, everybody seems to have his or her own charity, or development foundation. All of them try to raise funds from friends and family, all work for a better world. Along with a rising amount of nonprofits the importance of a watchdog increases. In the Netherlands the Central Bureau on Fundraising (CBF) is an independent foundation that has been monitoring fundraising by charities since 1925. Its' task is to promote trustworthy fundraising and expenditure by reviewing fundraising organizations and giving information and advice to government institutions and the public.

The number of registered ngo's went up from 832 to 1038 that shared more than €3 billion donated among them. It looks like the total funding reduced in numbers for 2011, but still the amount stays above the €3 billion, as far as it has been documented in October 2012. 811 Institutions raised a little less than half the funding themselves in 2010 (€1.412.591.783,33). Government subsidies counted for the rest of the

---

[244] Strategy & Society, The link between competitive advantage and corporate social responsibility, Porter & Kramer, Harvard Business Review, Dec 2006

amount. These were divided between 360 ngo's.

In 2010 the Gross Domestic Product (GDP) of the Netherlands was €588.4 billion. Foreign Aid amounted up to €4.6 billion in 2011. 23% of this money - more than €1 billion - was allocated through institutions such as Oxfam Novib, Hivos and ICCO, all three of them enlisted at CBF. The greatest part of Dutch spending on International Development remained governmental aid.[245]

Organizational capacity

Amongst the group of people who care for change and want to DO something, there also is a growing number of extreme wealthy former CEO's, such as Bill Gates (Microsoft) and Jeffrey Skoll (founder of E-bay). They set the mark, became role models and glamorized the change makers. They have been winners in the economic competition and are admired upon by many a businessman and corporate woman. These role models set out the track for a growing phenomenon: social entrepreneurship.

Social entrepreneurship has been a value for ages in Small and Medium sized Enterprises (SME) due to their local and regional roots. SME's are, by nature, interdependent of their direct environment. They employ their neighbours, they sell to their neighbours and, like dogs, they tend to keep their nest clean. Apart from this, SME's are agile and know what is relevant to their costumers, because the butcher talks to the vegetarian who lives next door and decides to take soya products into his assortment as well. For example.

Three business trends have come into sight:
1. Large organizations start to change from the inside, because they have to;
2. Co-operations add other values then profit to the way business is done;
3. Small and local by nature tends to take social and environmental issues into account and reacts with agility to changing (local) circumstances.

Companies, especially international businesses, have shown an amazing organizational capacity. They have built enormous factories in multiple

---

[245] See the website of Stichting Centraal Bureau Fondsenwerving (CBF)

countries, are continuously innovating production methods and procedures to stay in the game, plus they sell to consumers of all cultures and religions. For instance, Coca Cola can be found in every corner of the world. When in a country where potable water is hard to find, one can rely on Cola to drink. Where local and regional governments fail to up-scale, big business does it naturally. Once international companies obtain local roots and colour locale, they become agile and engaged like the SME's are by tradition. Then big business can combine the best of both worlds, for it is able to tackle many an issue that concerns a much larger geographic and social area. Child labour, for instance, or the water supply in a community.

Socializing business

The concept we referred to as conscious capitalism is gaining terrain. Ron Shaich, Panera Bread, witnessed on his own company. He socialized the Bakery Café chain as an asset, the way Porter and Kramer advised: beneficial for the company and for society. Shaich stated that putting donation boxes into the café instead of cash registers created sustainable business for the four pilot cafés the firm opened. Business has proven organizational capacity. Moreover large, multinational business has power that can be used for the benefit of society and business, such as is tried through the aforementioned Extractive Industries Transparency Initiative against corruption. The power of companies can be controlled by governments but is perhaps even more under the control of clients. The scrutiny of the citizen can break the reputation and shoot a hole into the profits - where it hurts most. On the other hand, this development evolves slow, too slow. Activism and conscious consumption are very necessary. In a different way from before. As Porter and Kramer stated rightfully activism and governments tend to behave suspicious towards the capitalist company, whereas the firm itself prefers to keep nosy parkers as far away as possible. This mutual distrust however is not getting either of them any further.

In the Dutch province of Noord-Brabant the regional government decided to bring the antagonists together, in search for mutual understanding and solving ecological issues. This program, called the Strategic Agenda, started ending the 1990's. Industry and environmental activists sat around the same table. There were discussions and even

dialogues. In the end, the rank and file of the diverse representatives did not go along, nothing changed, nobody took action. A failure?
Not in one, important, way: the key figures got to know each other. After the program was finished, they knew who was who in the other camp. They were on forename terms, drank a beer together. As a matter of fact some sort of consent started to sprout. This consent has grown through the years. Others, knowledge institutes, societal organizations et cetera, joined in. In 2012 Noord-Brabant has a strong infrastructure between organizations and individual people who know how to find each other and are able to talk solutions.

The same happened in the city of Rotterdam where the Rotterdam Climate Initiative joined parties that are natural opposites with opposite objectives. The port authorities of Europe's major port, employer's organization, SME's, builders, unions, heavy industries, university, colleges and city hall found an overall objective: a healthy prosperous green and clean city. Together they worked on this goal, keeping a keen eye on the profit, but understanding that ecological and societal bottom line, out of self-interest.

Exchange pleasure for joy
All the above are developments towards a joint effort society that include behaviour, decisionmaking and technology / institutionalization. These solutionfinding clusters operate together, influence each other and are reciprocal. They show a slow move towards a higher ecological, economic, socio-cultural and psychological level. The step forwards is so small, because it is not yet set by the majority. Society as a whole did not reach the point of self-awareness that is needed for a paradigm shift by the mainstream. How to arrive at such a level of awareness? The path will be paved by cooperation and wellbeing. One of the big mistakes society has made in terms of wellbeing, is that it replaced joy for pleasure, as was dictated by the marketing units of big business.

Joy is connected to blissful productivity. Joy, as Benedict Spinoza taught, is a condition of feeling joined to the creative unfolding of the most elementary human capabilities. Those who experience joy learn and become more and more active.
Gautama Buddha knew how to come to enlightenment and joy, Mahatma Ghandi found it out and Spinoza lectured it. These are all

men from distant ages, who have shared their thoughts and experiences in books that are still available to us, and still humanity in general hasn't found the way for all individuals to gain access to joy - to a life one has reason to value. The difficulty lies in the fact that these processes are individual processes, and we are seven billion individuals accumulating in numbers every second. The tipping point that turns joy into a mainstream ambition is not yet found. This has to do with the interrelations between society and individuals, with the social character Fromm wrote about and the dominating societal value To Have. However, there is reason for hope today. A lot has to do with the social media and game technology that spread news fast. Jane McGonigal[246] held a speech on TED in 2010 explaining the benefits of virtual gaming[247]. She wondered how the energy and creativity of 500 million gamers could be turned into a solutionfinding force. Gamers, she said, share four characteristics:

1. Urgent optimism (self-motivation)
2. Social Fabric (mutual trust and support)
3. Blissful productivity (happy to work hard)
4. Epic meaning (pursuing inspiring missions)

The problem with gamers is that they feel connected, self assured and active attracted to solving seemingly unsolvable issues online, but not in real life!

One of the reasons gamers are super empowered hopeful individuals is the feedback from a game: + 1 for writing a book, + 1 for speaking in public et cetera. Next to this is the possibility of an Epic Win, a gain that is almost impossible and still achieved. Gaming makes one feel good about him- or herself. From TED.com: 'Games like World of Warcraft give players the means to save worlds, and incentive to learn the habits of heroes. What if we could harness this gamer power to solve real-world problems? Jane McGonigal says we can, and explains how.' McGonigal designed games to solve the large issues such as oil

---

[246] Jane McGonigal (1977) is an American game designer, specialized in pervasive gaming and alternate reality games (ARGs). She currently serves as the Director of Game Research & Development at Institute for the Future and Chief Creative Officer at SuperBetter Labs. McGonigal has taught game design and game studies at the San Francisco Art Institute and the University of California, Berkeley.
[247] Jane McGonigal, Gaming can make a better world, Video on TED.com, 2010

peak, poverty and hunger, in an attempt to contribute to solutions together with all (and growing amount) gamers. Apart from understanding the gaming world, McGonigal knew about motivation and capabilities. In a game one can develop his or her capabilities unlimited.

How come our children spend 10.000 hours in gaming voluntarily, fully concentrated and learning on the job, while their school time is filled with an equal amount of hours, but perceived as boring and parents and teachers have to force the youth to study? How come that kids as old as four years can reproduce unspeakable names, the number of levels, how to reach these levels and what tools are needed, for imaginary game figures, while they seem unable to remember name of the capital of Denmark? Is reality more boring than the game world, or is it the way we teach?

The kids learn the complex games because they enjoy tackling the problems their avatars encounter. They fight the enemy together, in online games. They even cooperate with complete strangers. When you are on the verge of an epic win, you feel a life, productive and happy.

Intermezzo

A seventeen year old Dutch girl graduated from grammar school in the summer of 2011. She had obtained the highest possible grade in the Netherlands – gymnasium, learned Greek and Latin. She is an easy study and actually hardly opened a book in the six years she spent at grammar school.

Now she had to make a choice: further education or looking for a job. She did not know. She had no clue of who she was or wanted to become. On the Internet she discovered an anthroposophic school. This school offered an 'inbetween' year, for orientation and development of the self. A year that would be dedicated to finding out who you are becoming, through philosophy, sociology, ethics, studying the different religions. Plus through performing the diverse arts: dance, music, writing, theatre, painting and/or sculpting. This is where she went. The first weekend she came home, she was excited as well as deadly tired. 'I am so busy! And I like it all. I learn so much. And I am completely myself. For the first time in my life I feel happy and learning at school!'

What happened is that she discovered blissful productivity. She found out what being active is and what joy means. She got positive feedback and trust from the teachers and other students. There was a profound freedom to choose that liberated her. And she started to take responsibility for her own learning, her own actions and her own life. Now isn't this what we have to teach at every school, every level?[248]

Reason to value

The UNDP Human Development Report 2011 wrote: 'Human development is the expansion of people's freedoms and capabilities to lead lives that they value and have reason to value. It is about expanding choices. Freedoms and capabilities are a more expansive notion than basic needs. Many ends are necessary for a "good life," ends that can be intrinsically as well as instrumentally valuable - we may value biodiversity, for example, or natural beauty, independently of its contribution to our living standards'.[249] The UNDP referred to Amartya Sen and Sudhir Anand when it came to integrating Planet and People in development. People who have no access to potable water, for instance, are deprived in more than one way, since these people - in practice - are poor and vulnerable to abuse.

Sen, as well as Martha Nussbaum, made a strong case for a capability approach that must lead to freedom for all. Sen was the founding president of the Human Development and Capability Association, launched in September 2004. 'The HDCA promotes research from many disciplines on key problems including poverty, justice, wellbeing, and economics. Mission Statement: The Human Development and Capability Association (HDCA) shall promote high quality research in the interconnected areas of human development and capability. It shall be concerned with research in these areas across a broad range of topics where the human development and capability approaches have made and can make significant contributions, including the quality of life, poverty, justice, gender, development and environment inter alia. It shall further work in all disciplines - such as economics, philosophy, political theory, sociology and development studies - where such research is, or may be, pursued. While primarily an academic body, the Association shall bring together those primarily involved in academic work with practitioners who are involved in, or interested in, the application of

---

248 From family life
249 UNDP, Human Development Report 2011, Summary, p.7

research from the fields of human development and capability to the problems they face.'[250]

Martha Nussbaum was president of the HDCA from 2006-2008. She felt the need for a more comprehensive explanation of the capability approach and wrote the book Creating Capabilities, The Human Development Approach in 2011. The Capability Approach can be defined as an approach of human development that starts with the questions: 'Who can people really be? What can they really do? Which are the real capabilities people have at their disposal?'
These are substantive freedoms and a series of (often interrelated) opportunities to choose and act. Amartya Sen wrote the first sentence of the introduction of Development as Freedom[251]: 'Development can be seen, it is argued here, as a process of expanding the real freedoms that people enjoy.' Development in the eyes of Nussbaum and Sen is not confined to the poor(er) countries. All countries are developing countries, since in the whole world not one country has been able to realize dignity and equivalent opportunities for everybody inside its borders.[252]

Touching the essence of life
A person who ponders 'Who can I really be? 'What can I really do?' and, What are the substantive freedoms and opportunities I can choose and do?' realizes these are questions touching the essence of life. The awareness of the asker is raised just by asking those questions. Trying to find an answer by acting and living lifts the lit on the Joy jar if only a little. These questions concern being, not having. A palliative nurse from Australia, Bronnie Ware, who took care of dying people for a number of years, collected the regrets of life.

The five most common regrets are[253]:
1. I wish I'd had the courage to live a life true to myself, not the life others expected of me;
2. I wish I didn't work so hard;
3. I wish I'd had the courage to express my feelings;

---

[250] See Mission statement Human Development and Capability Association
[251] Amartya Sen, Development as Freedom, Oxford University Press, 1999
[252] Martha Nussbaum, Mogelijkheden scheppen, AMBO, 2012, p.35
[253] Bronnie Ware, Inspiration and Chai, Regrets of the dying

4. I wish I had stayed in touch with my friends;
5. I wish I had let myself be happier.

The regrets of the dying are expressions of not having been able to become who they are, to do what they really needed to do. These are shortages of capabilities. These people felt they hadn't lived the live they had reason to value. And all these people put the blame on themselves. 'I was untrue, worked too hard, didn't express myself, lost touch and / or denied myself happiness'. In the end we stand trial to nobody but ourselves. We feel accountable for our own (lack of) deeds.

The poem Instantes, contributed by some to the Argentine writer and poet Jorge Luis Borges (1899 – 1986) mourns the same mistakes. It ends like this[254]:

If I could live over again
I would go barefoot,
beginning in early spring
and would continue so until the end of autumn.
I would take more turns on the merry-go-round.
I would watch more dawns
and play with more children,
if I once again had a life ahead of me.
But, you see, I am eighty-five
and I know that I am dying.

The essence life is To Be. The capability approach of Sen and many more developing and economic theories contain aspects of being and include rights as the right to be lazy, the right to play, the right to enjoy. It is true that there is no country in the world yet that approaches its' citizens from the capability point of view.
When there are rights there are plights, some will argue. Still, plights are unnecessary when pushed on the right button.

The right button
Jane McGonigal showed how it works in games. Gamers are unpaid, very productive, voluntary workers, happy to spend their time solving

---

254 Instantes, last strophe, attr. to Jorge Luis Borges

gigantic problems. They don't feel abused, they feel blissful productive while on an epic mission.

McGonigal was participant architect of some world changing games. One of those, Urgent Evoke, a crash course changing the world, addressed enormous issues such as social innovation, food security, water crisis and, power shift, especially in Africa[255]. It was designed for the youth, funded by among others the World Bank, to get more people actively involved in sustainable progress. The game is built like a classic game, addressing the gamer as Hero, giving feedback in the form of +1 capabilities, creating suspense and secrecy as well as epic meaning: YOU CAN SAVE THE WORLD.

Ten missions were launched during ten weeks. Participation was free of charge. The gamer chose his or her own mission, for example social innovation. The gamer than entered level one: 'Master the mindset of a social innovator'. Here points could be achieved for learning for example. Social innovators, Urgent Evoke stated, have 33 secrets. 'Choose your secret, write a blog about it and own it. This will get you +1 Learn.' Especially the owning is interesting… the game tried to seduce the gamer to internalize the info. The secrets that were revealed contained principles on social innovation from a number of experts. The gamer was obtaining extra capabilities to tackle the problem and, was likely to use these in daily offline live as well. Plus, he or she shared ideas and knowledge with other gamers who were on the same journey. They cooperated in the true sense of the word, shared thoughts and ideas, fears and hopes without reservation. A school example of triple loop (accumulative) learning.

An earlier game, World Without Oil[256], dispersed information to the participants who were playing the first 32 weeks after a sudden global oil shortage. They got messages of food shortages, fights over resources et cetera. And they started to live as if there was no oil around, reporting about it in various ways, sharing, adapting to changed circumstances. Growing vegetables in kitchen gardens, commuting by bike et cetera, were among the solutions.
1500 People participated actively. Three years later, they still had the

---

255 Urgent Evoke, online game to save the world
256 World Without Oil, online game imagining the first 32 weeks of a global oil crisis

changed lifestyles they adopted when they were playing the future. It lowered their footprints, made them more aware and brought joy. 'Play it before you live it' is one of the slogans the alternate reality game goes by. There is a point to that.

If gamers can do it, why can't the rest of us?
Because writers experience the same optimism, blissful productivity and epic meaning when on the verge of writing the Best Book Ever. Even the social fabric has become important part of writing, since people can be working on the same document at the same time and the social media took a flight. Musicians, sporters, event organizers, scientists, explorers, doctors have equal inspiring experiences.
What Jane McGonigal showed, is common human characteristic; All people, gamers or not, want to lead productive, meaningful lives. Ask a child what she wants to become when she's grown up. She will always give an answer that refers to something she perceives as special and meaningful. She'll never tell you she wants to be unemployed. People strive for the fulfilling of their capabilities, from birth to death - the only reason they do not achieve their ambitions is: accommodation. A schoolteacher who says you will neverever master a certain subject. A parent that pushes you in a direction that is not fitting your personality. Or, an illness that prevents you from being active like you would want to be. Other deprivations, such as lack of education opportunities, and even more basic, lack of healthy food and potable water, a dangerous environment et cetera, have impacts on people's lives.

When people are allowed capabilities and develop awareness, they use their abilities and create. Individuals, all individuals, put effort into life and society by nature. The acting inspires them. A productive life using all capabilities one has, leads to meaningful wellbeing and joy.
In theory it is simple, push the right button and people start to behave more sustainable out of themselves.
Imagine a society in which every individual lives the life he or she has reason to value. Will people stop working? Yes. For, as Confucius said: 'Choose a job you love and you will never have to work a day in your life'.

Conclusion

The paradigm shift

For more than two-hundred years the dominant groups in society have put the emphasis on profits. They covered up greed with economical equations, arguing that in the end all (also the poor and the environment) would benefit from seeping down wealth. Competition was at the centre of the societal value system. The capitalist system would lead to a sound societal model. It appeared a completely wrong and destructive assumption.

Recently, at the fin de siècle, the ecology - Planet - slipped into political and economic ideologies. This was a very reluctant entrance, only allowed because resource depletion threatened to lower the profits. The P of People stayed in the niche all that time, with the exception of some welfare states - that took care of their own, only their own - and companies that needed skilled and motivated workers.

At this point in time, starting the second millennium, the catastrophes of the winner-takes-all mentality have reached frightening proportions. The great divide of today is that between Haves and Have Nots. The last group is growing by the day, not in the least caused by ecological disasters. Inequality is the time bomb human society is sitting on, enforced by environmental threats that will not stay confined to the deprived.

The most convenient and rational action is to pull out the fuse by ending the competition. Inequality can be erased by cooperation, sharing and accumulative learning. Cooperation requires a different attitude than competition, moreover it leads to more durable solutions.

JES! proposes a spiritual revolution, because when the brain shifts, reality shifts too. When multiple brains shift, society shifts too. Such a shift occurs through (self)awareness of the individual and profound compliance with human rights and fundamental human needs.
The economy is for the people, not vice verse and is embedded in the ecology and sociology. Economics is no more and no less than sound household management, which serves the purpose of people's development and wellbeing and can never be an end in itself.

The solutionfinding clusters - decisionmaking, behaviour and institutionalization / technology - can contribute to a rising level of wellbeing for all people. The aim is to create a joint effort society, where all individuals are equal and freely associate into the new political engagement model.

The approach that leads towards a joint effort society is called ecolution. It involves a transition towards a higher ecological, economic, social and psychological level that takes the wellbeing of 7 billion people into account each time we act.

The theory of ecolution offers a new conceptual framework, toolbox and method in the form of a dynamic matrix. It supports growing awareness and inspires different thinking and acting.

Inspiration and aspiration lead people to higher grounds. The inspiration for JES! was found in philosophy and literature. Aspiration came through observations and experiences of the authors that engaged in many a societal battle for equality, variety, empowerment and healthy life-supporting systems.

Summary

The overall convenient action

We are having a war against the poor, a war by the comfortable against the unfortunate[257]
J.K. Galbraith

The war between rich and poor is going on since 250 years ago global wealth rocketed onto a nearly vertical growth curve that we are still climbing today. The creation of wealth by a mix of technologies and organizational capacity of human beings during the Industrial Revolution was accompanied by increasing inequality. Social Darwinism introduced the concept of 'survival of the fittest' in order to justify class inequalities, racism, colonialism and other social injustices. Simultaneously mankind plundered the earth and destroyed all kinds of lifecycles.

The Industrial Revolution not only caused a civil war on global scale between rich and poor, but also a war of humanity against nature and in the end of human beings as a species against their own. Since the Industrial Revolution started in England - after which it became a world hit - humanity failed to resist the inner destructive powers and expressed this in behaviour, technologies, institutes, decisionmaking, procedures, cultures and social orders.

Despite good intentions and significant advances mankind failed to solve growing ecological, economic, social and psychological problems on global scale. Worldwide we didn't temper the population growth enough. We didn't share enough. We didn't learn and we didn't join efforts enough so everybody on Earth can lead a life of a meaningful wellbeing. We failed to conserve resources and to safeguard life-supporting eco-systems. We didn't secure the clean water supply, didn't stop the decline of bio-diversity, and were unsuccessful at beating slavery, educating children, banning arms and preventing wars.
We can blame it on the system, on our grandparents who took wrong decisions, but that doesn't help. After all, the systems, processes,

---

[257] Dr. John Kenneth Galbraith spring 1996, interview with the International Harvard Review

structures and cultures that have put us on the slope to destruction are self-made. Now we'll have to use our fantasy, creativity, energy and willpower to steer the whole development into a sustainable direction. This will not be easy. Systems are hard to steer. Especially the bottom up type which can be defined as a rhizome. One cannot predict the outcome of interventions. Therefore intervening requires sensitivity, agility and flexibility, but above all awareness.

One of the systems that got out of control and swept ecological and social fabrics along is the economic. Economists have been on the look-out for equilibrium of demand and supply for 250 years. Such free market equilibrium, brought to existence by the Invisible Hand, would take care of a fair distribution of goods.

However, there is one big problem: the economic system is open to a variety of influences (impulses, greed, irrational decisions, fears) and as a consequence permanent out of balance. As soon as one market tends to balance, it is thrown off again by another market. In the real world rational expectations and forecasts don't make sense. People are guided by animal spirits that disorganize, disorder and deconstruct the linear models that economists have built. Tensions and vibrations have more to do with psychology, biology and quantum mechanics. Nothing is fixed or certain, especially not in a complex world. Disequilibrium is the rule and equilibrium is the rare exception.

The current situation requires different axioms, paradigms and attitudes. Climate change and mass deprivation do not stop at borders or at the fence of a gated community. There is much to gain for the so-called winners as well as for losers.

Today the overall convenient action is not fight & divide but work together & unite. Cooperation leads to different paradigms on sharing and accumulative learning. It enhances social fabrics and is more likely to come up with durable solutions for the current global issues than competition and the free market mechanism. The latter encourage a fight of all against all, leaving us - mankind - as losers.

In a cooperative environment, the economy becomes embedded in and supportive of social and ecological goals, as it should be. Cooperation is one of the concepts that can add new meaning to being part of a society.

The movement away from competition replaces the Affluent Society with a new political engagement model: the Joint Effort Society. A joint effort society is a free association of individuals. All contribute, cooperate and co-create according to their ability and out of free will and all reap the fruits. Such a society has a healthy relationship with nature, understands the interconnectedness and reciprocity of systems and aims at the wellbeing of all people, here and now, there and later. The incremental progress to higher levels of wellbeing is called ecolution.

Ecolution imposes changes in the direction of a joint effort society. The theory of ecolution is based on the principle idea that changes are brought about by deconstruction. Dissent, diversity, variety and disorder prevent or stop the slack that is the presentiment of any system - a society, company, even the body and mind of a single person. The power to differ averts falling into the destruction phase.
Ecolution is the type of deconstruction that leads to a higher ecological, economic, social and psychological level each time a person or organization acts. Vigilant individuals and growing awareness are crucial. A society is created by the people in it, as much as the people are the product of their society. The theory of ecolution therefore approaches both sides: the whole and the individual.

The theory of ecolution contains a conceptual framework, toolbox and method to interfere when, or before, a system develops destructive tendencies. The approach is comprised in a model for strategy and vision creation that is dynamic and sensitive, always on the move, checking and balancing and that allows to decide on shared principles what to do to transform a development and reach towards a higher level of wellbeing for all.

This book is a call for positive action. JES! Towards a Joint Effort Society describes the context of today and comes up with concepts (plans for action) to deconstruct and change destruction into construction. In system language: it learns people and organizations to look for lever points (deconstruction) that take the wellbeing of more than 7 billion people to a higher level each time we act.

The trend towards a joint effort society is already visible in the niche of society, in the conceptual framework of organizations like the EU and the UN and in the workings and doings of many individuals and communities. These are the promising sprouts for the future.

Now let's act!

Acknowledgements

JES! started as a translation in English of the thesis Allemaal Winnen Frank co-authored. The original idea came from Donald Huisingh[258] whose enthusiasm fused the project. Allemaal Winnen researched regional sustainable development, using the Dutch province Noord-Brabant as a study case. Together with Martin Bakker, Frank designed a matrix, toolbox and new conceptual framework for development called ecolution. Donald thought the book should be available to other than Dutch readers as well.

Most writers and thinkers will agree that translating old work is not so much fun as coming up with something new. We already were beyond Allemaal Winnen. Therefore we decided to take the beef out of it - matrix, toolbox, conceptual framework - and apply these to the world, while improving on the theory and walking the talk.

Donald kept pace, more than that, he kept inspiring and being critical. Founding father of the Dutch Association of Integral Biological Architects, VIBA, Peter Schmid[259] did the same. These two mentors and friends were, and still are, with us all the way, providing insights, advice and recommending books to read.

We also have to thank our children, adopted children, friends and family for providing us with real life opportunities to apply the theory of a joint effort society. Many diners that have been devoted to discussing JES! and theories have been applied as try-out, sometimes more successful than others.

The people surrounding us are a bunch of mavericks, freedom fighters, musicians, artists, moviemakers, ict-ers, entrepreneurs, writers and thinkers. Together they form an international community without borders. Some are very young, others already reached a respectable age, but all are young in spirit. Not in the least our parents. Jan and Riet van

---

[258] Prof. Donald Huisingh, Institute for a Secure and Sustainable Environment, University of TN, Knoxville, USA.
[259] Prof. Emeritus TU/e Mag. Arch. Eng. Dr.h.c. Peter Schmid, R E D ResearchEducationDesign in ScienceArtTechnology for PeacefulSustainableDevelopment

Empel, who at the age of 88 supported in more than one way. Joost and Helma Sicking, who no longer inhabit this planet, have left us their ideals and works of art that still inspire.

Not in the least we thank you, reader, for your interest. We hope you will join us on the journey to a joint effort society. Please do share your thoughts, comments and questions with your friends and with us, so we can improve JES! and make it happen.

Frank van Empel & Caro Sicking

frank@nonfixe.nl
caro@nonfixe.nl

January 2014, Vught, The Netherlands

Bibliography

(n.d.). From World without Oil: http://worldwithoutoil.org

(n.d.). From Urgent Evoke: http://www.urgentevoke.com

Aletta Jacobs. (2013). *vrouwenkiesrecht*. From www.alettajacobs.org: http://www.alettajacobs.org/atria/Aletta_Jacobs/themas/vrouwenkiesrecht

Ayad, C. (2011 11-June). La Révolution de la Gifle. *La Libération* .

Bacile, S. (2012 14-September). Innocence of Muslims.

Bakker, M., & Empel, F. v. (2012). *Allemaal Winnen, regionale duurzame ontwikkeling (Ecolutie)*. Rotterdam, The Netherlands: Erasmus University and Studio nonfiXe.

Bangasser, P. (2000). *The ILO and the informal sector: an institutional history*. International Labour Organisation.

Bateson, G. (1979). *Mind and Nature, a necessary unity*. E.P. Dutton.

Beinhocker, E. (2007). *The Origin of Wealth; Evolution, Complexity and the Radical Remaking of Economics*. Random House Business Books.

Borges, J. (n.d.). Instantes.

Brecht, B. *Dreigroschen Oper*.

Bryan, B., Goodman, M., & Schaveling, J. *Systeemdenken*. The Hague, The Netherlands: Academic Service, Sdu Uitgevers.

Centraal Bureau Fondsenwerving (CBF). (n.d.). From www.cbf.nl.

Central Planning Agency. (2012). *Actualization Dutch Economy until 2018, plans of the VVD/PvdA-government included*. The Hague.

Chamberlain, G. (2012 4-August). India targets the traffickers who sell children into slavery. *The Guardian / The Observer* .

Chandler, A. (1994). *Scale and Scope*. Harvard University Press.

Chopra, D., & Rudolph, T. (2012). *Super Brain*. Rider.

Cialdini, R. (2001). *Invloed, theorie en praktijk*. Uitgeverij Nieuwezijds.

Cradle to Cradle. (2009 January). *Project Almere*. From http://www.cradletocradle.nl: http://www.cradletocradle.nl/home/818_almere.htm

Crawshaw, S., & Jackson, J. (2010). *Small Acts of Resistance*. Sterling Publishing Co.

Darwin, C. (2001). *Over het Ontstaan der Soorten*. (L. Hellemans, Trans.) Uitgeverij Nieuwezijds.

Dean, L., Kendal, R., Schapiro, S., Thierry, B., & Laland, K. (2012). Identification of the Social and Cognitive Processes Underlying Human Cumulative Culture. *Science* , *335* (1114).

Deutsch, M. (1999). *A Personal Perspective on Social Psychology*.

Dierickx, G. (2005). *De logica van de politiek*. Uitgeverij Garant.

Dobson, A. (Ed.). *The Green Reader*.

Dubashi, P. (2008). Critique of Neo-classical Economics. *Mainstream* , *XLVI*.

Ekins, P., & Max-Neef, M. (Eds.). (1992). *Real-Life Economics: Understanding Wealth Creation.* London, UK: Routledge.

Elkington, J. (1999). *Cannibals with Forks. Triple Bottom line of 21th century business.* New Edition.

Empel, F. v. (1997). *Model Holland.* Dutch Social Partners.

Empel, F. v., & Sicking, C. (2007 June). Motivation. *4P - Investors in People* .

Empel, F. v., & Sicking, C. (2011). *Power Essays.* Vught, The Netherlands: Province of Noord-Brabant and Studio nonfiXe.

European Court for Human Rights (ECHR). (2013). *The Court in Brief.* From http://www.echr.coe.int: http://www.echr.coe.int/Pages/home.aspx?p=court

Fennema, M. *De moderne democratie.*

Feyerabend, P. (2011). *The Tyranny of Science.* Polity Press.

Fisher, F., & Forrester, J. (1993). *Rein and Schön, Reframing policy discourse.* UCL Press.

Flemons, D. *May the Pattern be With You, Cybernetics and Human Knowing.*

Forbes. (2013). OESO-data from 182 countries.

Forrester, J. (197). *World Dynamics.* Cambridge: Wright-Allen Press.

Frenken, K. (2012 22-October). Jongere wil auto wel delen en dat is winst. *Trouw* .

Friedman, M. (1970 13-September). The social responsibility of business is to increase its profits. *The New York Times Magazine* .

Fromm, E. (1987). *Een kwestie van Hebben of Zijn, grondslagen voor een nieuwe levensoriëntatie in de consumptiemaatschappij* (3rd Edition ed.). Utrecht, The Netherlands: Bijleveld.

Galbraith, J. (1987). *The Nature of Mass Poverty.* Pelican Books.

Gladwell, M. (2005). *Blink.* Back Bay Books.

Goldstein, E. (2012). *Before the Arab Spring, the unseen thaw.* World Report, Human Rights Watch.

Guattari, G. D. (2008). *A Thousand Plateaus, Capitalism and Schizophrenia.* Continuum.

Gunsteren, H. (2006). *Vertrouwen in democratie, Over de principes van zelforganisatie.* Amsterdam: van Gennep.

Gylfason, T. (2010). Natural Resource Endowment: A Mixed Blessing? *Seminar on Natural Resources, finance and development, Central Bank of Algeria and IMF Institute.* Algiers.

Herpen, M. v. (2006). Ecologisch Verantwoord Onderwijs. *Dertig jaar ErvaringsGerichtOnderwijs* .

Hochschild, A. (2012). *King Leopold's Ghost, a story of greed, terror and heroism in colonial Africa* (2nd Edition ed.). Pan Books.

Hugo, V. (1849). My Revenge is Fraternity. Paris, France.

Human Development and Capability Association. (2013). *History and Mission.* From http://hd-ca.org/: http://hd-ca.org/about/hdca-history-and-mission

International Labour Office and International Programme on the Elimination of Child Labour. (2007). *Modern Policy and Legislative Responses to Child Labour*.

International Labour Organisation (ILO). (2010). *Accelerating against Child Labour*. Global ILO Report, ILO.

International Labour Organisation (ILO). (2013). *Mission and Objectives*. From www.ilo.org: http://www.ilo.org/global/about-the-ilo/mission-and-objectives/lang--en/index.htm

Ishay, M. (2004). *The History of Human Rights*. University of California Press.

Keane, J. (2010). *Life and Death of Democracy*. Edition Pocket Books.

Kennisplatform Verkeer en Vervoer. (2012 June). *KpVV Dashboard duurzame en slimme mobiliteit*. From http://kpvvdashboard-4.blogspot.nl: http://kpvvdashboard-4.blogspot.nl/2012/06/autodelen-aan-vooravond-van-doorbraak.html

Kogon, E. (1974). *Der SS-Staat, Das System der Deutschen Konzentrationslager*. München, Germany: Wilhelm Heyne Verlag.

Kolb, D. (1984). *Experimental Learning*.

Kolstoe, J. (1995). *Developing Genius*. Georg Ronald Publisher Ltd.

Korsten, A. (2005 11-March). From Arno Korsten: http://www.arnokorsten.nl/PDF/Beleid/Deliberatieve%20beleidsanalyse.pdf

Kotter, J. (1996). *Leading Change*. Harvard Business School Press.

Lijphart, A. (1984). *Democracies, Patterns of Majoritarian and Consensus Government in Twenty-One Countries*. Yale University Press.

Likert, R. (2013). From Social Research Methods: http://www.socialresearchmethods.net/kb/scallik.php

Lofting, C. (1999). *Market Games: the 'what' and the 'where' in the stock market*.

Lovins, A. (2011). *Reinventing Fire, bold business solutions for the new energy era*. Chelsea Green Publishing.

Lovins, A., Lovins, H., & Hawken, P. (2000). *Natural Capitalism, creating the next industrial revolution*. First Back Bay Paperback edition.

Lutz, R., Capra, F., Callenbach, E., & Marburg, S. *Innovations Ökologie*.

Main, J., & J., W. (1998). *Driving Change*. London, UK: Kogan Page.

Massey, R. (2012 2-February). Britains longest clutter free street unveiled makes things safer. *Daily Mail* .

Max-Neef, M. A. (1991). *Human Scale Development*. Apex Press.

Max-Neef, M. (2010 19-November). *Barefoot Economics part 2, Economy how it should be*. From Youtube: https://www.youtube.com/watch?v=MTIpWUvoQl4

Max-Neef, M., & P.B., S. (2012). *Economics Unmasked, from power and greed to compassion and the common good*. Green Books.

McGonigal, J. (2010 February). *Gaming can make a better world*. From http://www.ted.com: http://www.ted.com/talks/jane_mcgonigal_gaming_can_make_a_better_world?language=nl

Meadows, D. (2009). *Thinking in Systems*. Earthscan.

Moyo, D. (2009). *Dead Aid*. Allen Lane.

Mywheels. (2014). *veel gestelde vragen.* From https://mywheels.nl:
https://mywheels.nl/hoe-autodelen-werkt/veel-gestelde-vragen#show
Nederlands Juristen Comité voor de Mensenrechten. (2010 9-April). *Uitspraak Hoge Raad in SGP zaak.* From www.njcm.nl:
http://www.njcm.nl/site/jurisprudentie/show/54
nonfiXe, the Power to Differ. (2013). From www.nonfixe.nl:
http://www.nonfixe.nl/wp-content/uploads/2013/08/Circus-in-Ethiopië-financiële-bijdrage-Oxfam-Novib.pdf
Nussbaum, M. (2012). *Mogelijkheden Scheppen.* AMBO.
Oger, E. (2006). *Derrida, een inleiding.* Uitgeverij Klement.
Panizzon, M. (2012). *Diaspora for Development in Africa, France's Codevelopment Program: Financial and Fiscal Incentives to Promote Diaspora Entrepreneurship and Transfers.* World Bank.
Parliament UK. (2013 10-April). *Tributes to Baroness Thatcher at the House of Commons.* From www.parliament.uk:
http://www.publications.parliament.uk/pa/cm201213/cmhansrd/cm130410/debtext/130410-0001.htm
Pillay, N. (2011). *Declaration on the Right to Development at 25.* From
http://www.un.org: http://www.un.org/en/events/righttodevelopment/
Porter, M., & Kramer, M. (2011 January). Creating Shared Value. *Harvard Business Revue* .
Porter, M., & Kramer, M. (2006 December). Strategy & Society, The link between competitive advantage and corporate social responsibility. *Harvard Business Review* .
Reybrouck, D. v. (2010). *Congo.* De Bezige Bij.
Ruttan, V., & Hayami, Y. (2011). *Can Economic Growth Be Sustained?* (K. Otsuka, & C. Ford Runge, Eds.) Oxford University Press.
Sartre, J. *Over het Existentialisme.* Utrecht, The Netherlands: AW Bruna & Zoon.
Savater, F. (1999). *Het goede leven; Ethiek voor mensen van morgen* (5th Edition ed.). Utrecht, The Netherlands: Bijleveld.
Schumacher, E. (1977). *A Guide for the Perplexed.* Harper Perennial.
Schumacher, E. (1973). *Small is Beautiful, Economics as if People Mattered.* Harper Perennial.
Schumacher, E. (2007). Summary of The Age of Plenty. (R. Krishnan, Ed.) *A Survey of Ecological Economics* .
Sen, A. (1999). *Development as Freedom.* Oxford University Press.
Sen, A. (2010). *The Idea of Justice.* Penguin Books.
Shaich, R. (2011 28-October). *Corporations must become Socially Conscious Citizens.* From Harvard Business Review Blog Network:
http://blogs.hbr.org/2011/10/corporations-must-become-socia/
Sicking, C. (2010 7-December). *Freedom of Speech.* From www.nonfixe.nl:
http://www.nonfixe.nl/freedom-of-speech/
Sicking, C. (2012). *nonfixe blogspot.* From http://nonfixe.blogspot.nl:

http://nonfixe.blogspot.nl/2012/09/pakistans-black-law.html

Smith, A. (1976). *The Wealth of Nations*. Penguin Books.

Snyder, G. (2000). *The Gary Snyder Reader, The 'East-West' Interview*. Counterpoint.

Sociale Economische Raad (SER). (2013). From About SER:
http://www.ser.nl/en/about_the_ser.aspx

Spinoza, B. d. (1677). *On the Improvement of Understanding*.

Stiglitz, J., A., S., & Fitoussi, J. (2010). *Mis-measuring our lives, Why GDP doesn't add up*. The New Press.

Sunderland, J., & Farmer, A. (2012 17-October). EU, as peacemaker, should welcome those fleeing war. *European Voice* .

Sustainable Development Solutions Network (SDSN). (n.d.). *Vision and Organization*. From http://unsdsn.org: http://unsdsn.org/about-us/vision-and-organization/

Swieringa, J., & Wierdsma, A. (1992). *Op weg naar een lerende organisatie*.

The Natural Step. (n.d.). *The Four System Conditions*. From www.naturalstep.org:
http://www.naturalstep.org/en/the-system-conditions

Threesigma. (2009 20-October). *A Systems Thinking Primer*. From
http://threesigma.com

Tschumi, B. (2004). *Event Cities 3, Concept vs. Context*. Cambridge: MIT Press.

UNDP. (2011). Human Development Report.

United Nations. (1948). *The Universal Declaration of Human Rights*. From
http://www.un.org: http://www.un.org/en/documents/udhr/

Veneklasen, L., & Miller, V. (2007 March). *A New Weave, The Action Guide for Advocacy and Citizen Participation*. From http://www.justassociates.org:
http://www.justassociates.org/en/resources/new-weave-power-people-politics-action-guide-advocacy-and-citizen-participation

Vrijheid van Beweging. (2013). *Fort Nederland in Beeld*. From
www.vrijheidvanbeweging.nl:
http://www.vrijheidvanbeweging.nl/fortnederland/dc16.html

Vrijheid van Beweging. (2013). *Fort Nederland in Beeld*. From
www.vrijheidvanbeweging.nl:
http://www.vrijheidvanbeweging.nl/fortnederland/zestienhoven.html

Ware, B. (2009 19-November). *Regrets of the dying*. From Inspiration and Chai:
http://bronnieware.com/regrets-of-the-dying/

Whitehouse. (2012 1-July). *We The People*. From http://www.whitehouse.gov:
http://www.whitehouse.gov/blog/2012/10/15/blog-action-day-power-we

Willis, K. (2011). *Theories and Practices of Development* (2nd Edition ed.). Routledge.

Wolf, N. (2007). *The End of America, Letter of Warning to a Young Patriot, A citizen's call to action*. Canada: Chelsea Green Publishing Company.

World Bank. (2011). *Migration and Remittances Factbook*.

World Bank. (2012). *Remittance Markets in Africa*. (S. Mohapatra, & D. Ratha, Eds.)

World Bank. (2001). *World Bank Development Report*.

Your notes and drawings

*nonfi*Xe
the power to differ

*nonfi*X*e*
the power to differ

*nonfi**X**e*
the power to differ